KNIT
my skirt

candace
eisner
STRICK

WITHDRAWN

PHOTOGRAPHY BY Alexis Xenakis

D0943449

PUBLISHER • Alexis Yiorgos Xenakis

EDITOR • Elaine Rowley

MANAGING EDITOR • Karen Bright

TECHNICAL EDITOR • Rick Mondragon

PROOFER • Sarah Peasley

ART DIRECTOR • Natalie Sorenson

PHOTOGRAPHER • Alexis Yiorgos Xenakis

STUDIO PHOTOGRAPHER • Dennis Pearson

STYLIST & SKETCH ARTIST • Rick Mondragon

CHIEF EXECUTIVE OFFICER • Benjamin Levisay

TECHNICAL ILLUSTRATOR • Carol Skallerud

PRODUCTION DIRECTOR & COLOR SPECIALIST • Dennis Pearson

BOOK PRODUCTION • Greg Hoogeveen • Carol Skallerud

FIRST PUBLISHED IN THE USA
IN 2016 BY XRX, INC.

COPYRIGHT © 2016 XRX, INC.

All rights reserved.
ISBN 978-1-933-06481-9

Produced in Sioux Falls, South Dakota; by

XRX, Inc.
PO Box 965
Sioux Falls, SD
57101-0965 USA

605.338.2450

Visit us online — knittinguniverse.com

Printed in Hong Kong.

No part of this publication may be reproduced, stored in a retrieval system, or transmitted, in any form or by any means, electronic, mechanical, photocopying, recording or otherwise, without the prior permission of the copyright holder. The designs in this book are protected by copyright and may not be made for resale. We give permission to readers to phototcopy the instructions and graphics for personal use only.

my skirts

For Ken,
Still the same as when I first played the show:
"Strange, dear, but true, dear,
When I'm close to you, dear,
The stars fill the sky,
So in love with you am I."
– Cole Porter's *Kiss Me, Kate*

Skirts hold open the door to endless creativity;
they are a blank canvas on which to design shapes,
colors, stitch patterns, embellishments,
and construction techniques.

When XRX approached me about writing a book on skirts, I have to admit that I was overwhelmed with anticipation and joy.

I love big projects. I love to knit. I anticipated more than a year of designing, knitting, and working with beautiful yarn — three things that knitters universally dream about.

I started where almost all knitters would start … with yarn. This was my box of paints, and I was never disappointed with any color, fiber, or texture I received from all the companies who generously supplied me with yarn. Next came my blank canvas, where all the other decisions had to be made. Most of the time my mind would be racing so much that I feared I would have the brain equivalent of a heart attack — there was just too much to choose from. Those were the times when I had to step away from the yarn and the knitting and focus on narrowing my thoughts down to a few choices. I had to stay away from the drawing board and the tools and just think. Walking and riding my bike provided me with those blank blocks of time. Many decisions were made when I was lying in bed, trying to sleep. Some even came about while I was actually asleep.

KNIT my skirt

Eventually I would settle on my decisions and start the knitting. A lot of the designing came about on the needles, an original concept often changing right in the middle of a row.

Oh, the knitting! Skirt knitting is nirvana. I would reach the zone almost immediately, and the knitting was nothing but sheer pleasure. It went by in the blink of an eye, then came the final round and I was done. I stepped back to admire my masterpiece. I loved it, but almost immediately my brain kicked in with the "what ifs." From my days as a musician, these are what I call variations on a theme—I can honestly say that they are endless.

Almost all of the skirts in this book have a variation on a theme. Some are actually written out in pattern form for you; others are suggestions with the pattern. Changing the yarn and a few colors can give a totally different look, as with *My Look at it from All Angles Skirt,* page 110, and *My Diamonds and Jeans Skirt,* page 113 (where even the placement of those colors offers an endless variety of choices). Of course changing the length goes without much explanation. And a quick change to a skirt's bottom circumference can transform it from sleek and classically form-fitting to swingy Bohemian, as in the case of *My This Chick Means Business Skirt,* page 28 vs. *My La Bohème Skirt,* page 32.

If you thought you could never wear a knit skirt, think again. The huge range of fibers, styles, and fits will make any woman (or man) look fashionable and attractive. And another plus to knitting a skirt? Sleeves are optional!

my skirts

top down

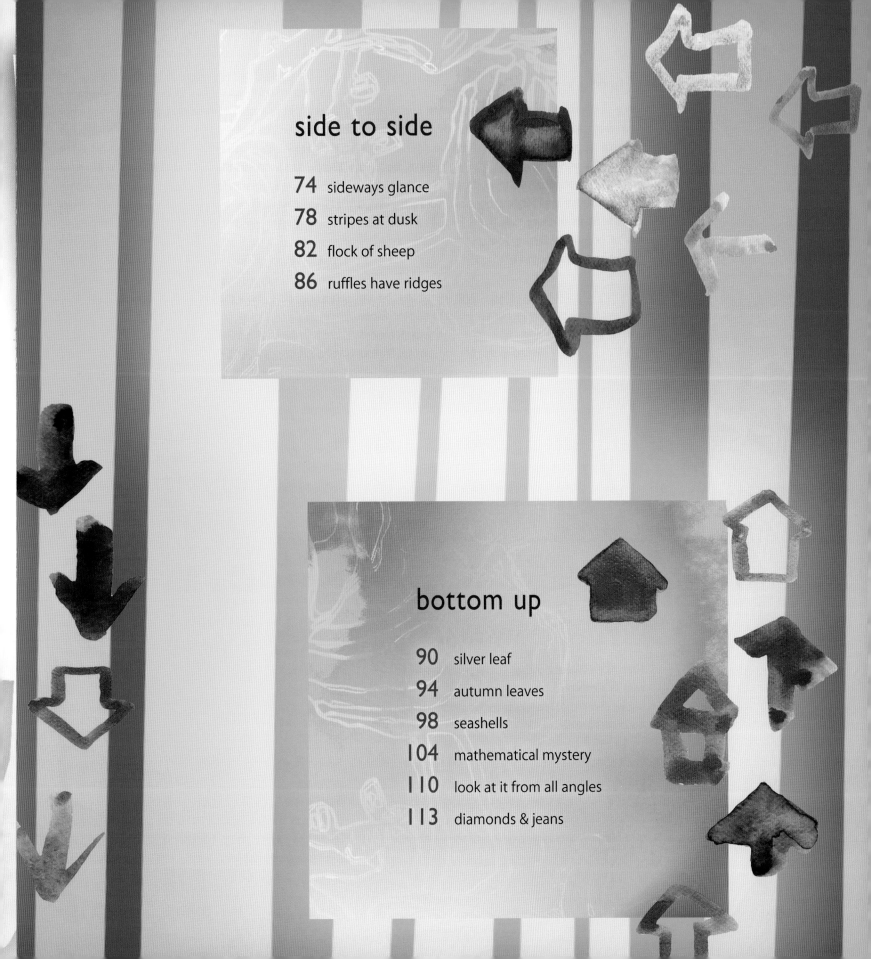

side to side

bottom up

{Continued from page 2}

made more difficult due to the yards and yards of fabric flowing all around them. Gradually, pants worked their way into women's wardrobes. For many women today, pants are almost exclusively their everyday, practical garb.

When you want the ultimate expression of femininity, it's still the skirt that comes out at the top of the list. Not the perfume, not the jewelry, not the ribbons in your hair, but the skirt. It is a fluid flow of fabric that cascades down your legs as far as you like, and that can have little elements of surprise put into the hemline, drawing the eye's attention down to those glorious shoes you bought to go with it. It is a swirl. It is a whisper. It is a seduction.

I love to wear skirts, so when I started to design them, knit them, and wear them, I was surprised to get negative feedback. The most frequent comment was, "I would never wear a knit skirt." A variation of this was "I *could* never wear a knit skirt." It seems that some women think they are going to look terrible in a knit skirt. As one said to me, "Every lump and bump is going to show." Yet pants are apt to highlight two areas of the body that women feel the most uncomfortable about — the tummy and the derrière. A well-fitting skirt knit in a beautiful fiber will skim over the body areas we are all acutely aware of, making for a smoother silhouette. It skirts our issues.

"I could never wear a knit skirt."

Contrary to what you may have heard, read, or told yourself, you CAN wear a skirt. A skirt will flatter the parts of you that pants won't. And a *knit* skirt can, too. Banish the image of those 1950s ribbed skirts. Today's knit skirts can be form-fitting if you wish, or swingy and beautifully draped — thanks to the vast variety of wonderful fibers now offered in yarn form.

I knit every one of the designs in this book and tried each one on when it was finished. While the measurements differed from design to design, I found that all of them fit me and all of them looked good. This worked because, even if the hip circumference — the most important number in a knit skirt — did not match mine, the very nature of the knit fabric compensated for that.

4

"It's going to seat out when I sit down and then stand up."

Yup, it WILL do that if you make it too tight. Allow an inch or two of ease and you will not have a problem. Many of the skirts in this book have no discernible front or back and can be rotated each time you put them on. This helps to even out any points of stress that might occur. Wearing a slip underneath also keeps stretching to a minimum. Some people like to sew a lining into the skirt, or will even purchase a half slip and sew that inside the waistband of the skirt. But for practicality and economy, you can buy one slip and wear it under all your skirts.

"I can't wear a skirt as my legs are horrible."

Of course you can wear a skirt! We are all our own worst critics. Make the skirt long enough so you feel comfortable. Maybe wear it with tights or a pair of leggings. I love the look and comfort of leggings, as I don't have to be aware of how I am sitting. I only wish they had been in fashion back when I played the cello in my miniskirts!

"It will take me forever to knit it."

You'd be surprised. As one of my colleagues put it, "It's a sweater without sleeves." And there is almost no finishing to do when the knitting is complete.

An average sweater in sport-weight yarn, knit to a gauge of 5–6 stitches per inch, uses about 1400 yards for a 36" finished chest measurement. A skirt in the same yarn for the same person (with a 28" waist and a 38" hip) would use, on average, 880 yards.

In fingering weight, a sweater for our size 36" person would use 1800 yards at a gauge of 6.5–7 stitches per inch. A skirt would use fewer than 1300 yards for the same person's lower half.

Of course this all depends on the shape of the skirt, the stitch pattern, and the length, but as a general rule, less yarn is used. Hence — less time to knit!

"I haven't worn a skirt since Junior High School. How will I know it will look good on me?"

The answer? Go shopping! But bring along a blank piece of paper, a pencil, a tape measure, and your camera. Try on skirts. When you find one you like, try on other skirts with similar silhouettes. Make a detailed schematic of the skirt that fits — lay it out on the floor of the dressing room and take measurements every few inches. Take pictures of it! If you really like it, just buy it — then you can do all of the above in the privacy of your own home. Next, knit a skirt with the same basic measurements. If you knit the skirt from the top down, you can try it on at any time, making easy adjustments along the way to ensure a perfect fit.

When someone asks, "What should I knit?" I would like the answer to be,

"Knit my skirt!"

1850 1860 1864 1868 1872 1877 1881 1887

WHAT I LEARNED FROM KNITTING

my first ♥ skirt

I bought beautiful linen yarn years ago, and after letting it age to perfection in my stash, decided it was perfect for a simple knit skirt pattern. The skirt started at the waist, a casing was knit for elastic, and the rest of the skirt was in stockinette stitch, with evenly spaced increases throughout, and a cute little lace pattern at the hemline.

The knitting was pleasurable and went quickly. I measured elastic to fit my waist and inserted it into the waistband. I eagerly tried on my new skirt, looked into the mirror and…my heart sank.

I said what every woman throughout history has said when looking at themselves in a full-length mirror: "I look fat." I have a strong premonition that somewhere in history a cave woman saw her reflection in a pond and said those same words.

It was true though. I *did* look fat. I had a huge ruffle of fat-like fabric around my waistline — too much material was gathered up by the elastic around my waist. Not to be thwarted by this, I took the skirt off, cut off the casing with the elastic in it, threw it out, and headed to Walmart.

I was in luck! They were having a huge sale on teenybopper tights with zippers down the outsides of the legs—$3.00 a pair, without tax. Back home, I cut the legs off the tights, leaving a smooth waistband attached to about 5" of stretchy fabric. Pulling it over the skirt's top (where the casing used to be), I sewed it on. Voila! I now had a skirt that fit and was smooth from my waist to my hips. The skirt was comfortable and flattering.

Next day I headed back to get more of those tights. Apparently there had a been a run on them, but I looked around and found several alternatives that had flat elastic waistbands and were reasonably priced. Since then I have used jersey-knit exercise shorts ($6), the tops of worn-out bike tights, and my latest: $2.96 underpants that are described as "undershapers." There are lots of economical choices out there—just look for something with a stretchy but smooth top. Avoid sweatpants, as they usually have a gathered elastic waistband or drawstring, but lots of exercise clothing does work well.

Besides the advantage of great fit, my repurposed tops also save on knitting, time, and yarn.

What did I learn from this disaster/success experience? The more fabric you have bunched around you, the fatter you look. We all think we need to "cover up" those problem areas, but the truth is, the more fabric you put around them, the more of a problem they become.

In this book, waist choices include a repurposed top, a drawstring, or elastic. All options allow for a few pounds in either direction, do not add bulk, and are comfortable to wear.

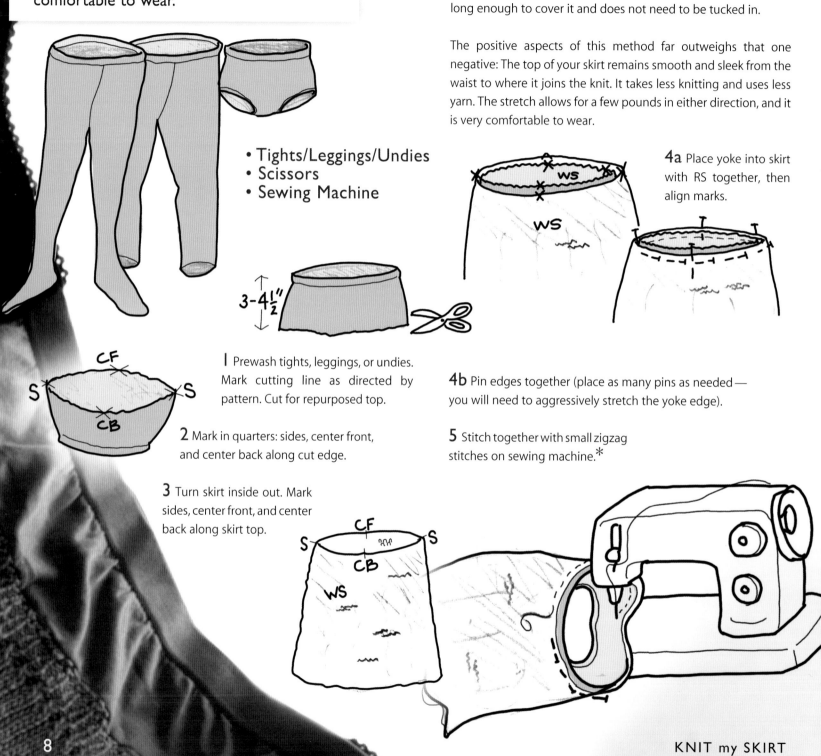

Repurposed top sewn to skirt

This is perhaps my favorite waist choice, even though it has one negative: it's functional, not decorative. Wear it with a top that is long enough to cover it and does not need to be tucked in.

The positive aspects of this method far outweighs that one negative: The top of your skirt remains smooth and sleek from the waist to where it joins the knit. It takes less knitting and uses less yarn. The stretch allows for a few pounds in either direction, and it is very comfortable to wear.

• Tights/Leggings/Undies
• Scissors
• Sewing Machine

3-4½"

1 Prewash tights, leggings, or undies. Mark cutting line as directed by pattern. Cut for repurposed top.

2 Mark in quarters: sides, center front, and center back along cut edge.

3 Turn skirt inside out. Mark sides, center front, and center back along skirt top.

4a Place yoke into skirt with RS together, then align marks.

4b Pin edges together (place as many pins as needed — you will need to aggressively stretch the yoke edge).

5 Stitch together with small zigzag stitches on sewing machine.*

*Should you lack access to a machine, you can hand sew. Just make sure to stitch at a rate similar to your knitting gauge. Herringbone stitch allows for ease, stretch, and give.

6 Turn right side out, wash and block.

If you wish to wear your skirt with the waistband showing, the following options using a drawstring or elastic are for you.

Drawstring options

Taking a hint from the sweatpants I told you to avoid, a drawstring is an easy way to make any skirt waist comfortable. A simple crocheted drawstring made with 2 strands of yarn held together can be woven through an eyelet row or round knit at the waist. This allows for easy adjustment if you want to share clothes, and also is good for periods of weight fluctuation.

Eyelet OVER AN EVEN NUMBER OF STITCHES
Eyelet row K1, **[k2tog, yo]** to last stitch, k1.
Eyelet round **[K2tog, yo]** to end of round..

chain stitch
1 Make a slip knot to begin. **2** Catch yarn and draw through loop on hook.

First chain made. Repeat Step 2.

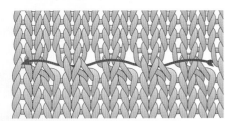

Weave a drawstring through eyelets.

The next 2 methods begin with a generous length of elastic. Attach the elastic to the waist of the skirt, try it on and adjust for fit, cut off the excess, overlap the ends, and sew together.

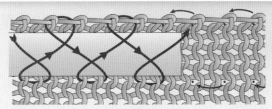

Work herringbone stitch over elastic.

Attaching elastic with herringbone stitch

While this may sound very similar to making a casing and inserting elastic through it, it actually is quicker to do and more flattering, as there is not the extra bulk of a casing plus the elastic around your waist. Use any width of elastic and work herringbone stitches over it. You can use the same yarn as the skirt, or, if that seems unwieldy, cut a length and remove and ply or two, leaving the number of plies that are comfortable to sew with.

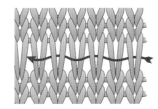

Weave elastic through elongated stitches.

Elongated-stitch casing

Using an elongated stitch at the waist allows for a quick knit casing, as in the case of My Little Black Skirt. The wider the elastic you wish to use, the longer the dropped stitches you need to encase the elastic — I usually yo 3 times.
    Round 1 Knit.
    Round 2 **[K1, yo 3 times]** to end of round.
    Round 3 Knit, dropping all yos from previous round.

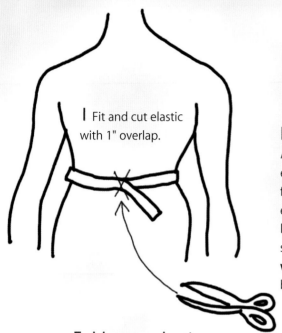

1 Fit and cut elastic with 1" overlap.

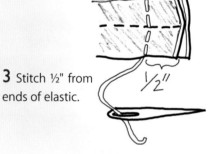

Fold-over elastic

A recent entry into the sewing market, fold-over elastic is perfect for a waistband. Apply it for a finished waistband in which the cast-on or bind-off is enclosed within the fold. It is hand-stitched to My Green Valley Skirt and looks sleek and crisp (page 57). Unfortunately, the color selection for home sewing is limited to black and white (with a few dyed colors available from **www.AlabamaChanin.com**). If the color works and you choose to tuck in a blouse, it is most attractive, otherwise it could be camouflaged with a belt.

- Fold-over elastic
- Button & carpet thread
- Scissors
- Sharp needle & pins

2 Fold in half with RS together.

3 Stitch ½" from ends of elastic.

4 Open seam.

5 Hide elastic in fold-over.

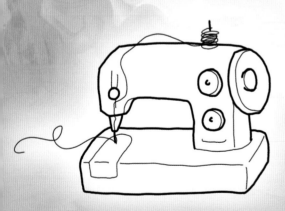

6 Open elastic band. Fold in half with seam at one side; mark halfway point (X).

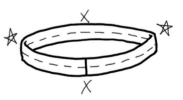

7 Fold in half again, matching halfway mark to seam; mark quarter points (✿).

10

KNIT my skirt

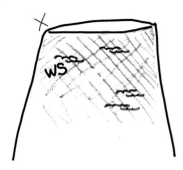

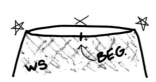

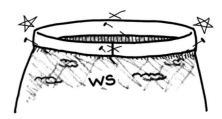

8 Turn skirt inside out. Lay flat with beginning of round at one side; mark halfway point.

9 Fold in half, matching halfway mark with beginning of row; mark ¼ points.

10 Tuck waist of skirt into folded elastic band as follows: Align elastic band seam with beginning of row/round. Align and pin halfway marks. Align and pin ¼ marks.

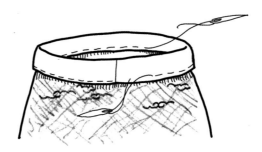

11 Stretch elastic to fit skirt and pin in place (you may want to pin on both RS and WS).

12 Baste in place on both sides.

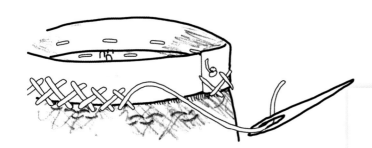

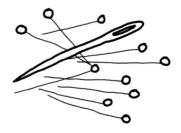

13 From WS, work herringbone stitch, catching both layers of elastic, with skirt waistband inside fold. Remove basting threads.

Next we'll look at taking the measurements and how to apply them to our 3 approaches to knit skirts: top down, bottom up and side-to-side.

your Skirt Plan

A STARTING POINT...

Presented in this book are three different construction blueprints for knitting a skirt—top down, bottom up, and side to side. While it may seem like a directional trilemma, each way has its own merits.

Top Down

A skirt knit from the waist to the hemline is my personal favorite, both to design and to knit. More than half of the skirts in this book are knit this way.

There are several other reasons I like this approach:

🔻 I have found that I can change my mind about many aspects of the skirt while right in the middle of the knitting,

🔻 You cast on fewer stitches at the top than you would at the bottom.

🔻 You can try the skirt on to see that all is going as planned—just put your stitches onto two or three circular needles, or onto a thread. I think it's important to try the skirt on every few inches until you're sure it's what you want. I know you know this already, but it is much less stressful to rip out 2" of work than 6"!

🔻 The flow of the construction is almost organic. Cast on the waist stitches and increase to the hip. Once the hip measurement is reached, you are pretty much free to do whatever you want—adding embellishments, changing colors, changing stitch patterns, etc. You can continue increasing at the same rate, at a different rate, or do no further increasing at all. Then, just knit to the desired length—the beauty of knitting any skirt from the top down is that you can end the knitting at the length that is right for you.

🔻 I usually find myself thinking about doing something different at the bottom than what I had originally planned. I love flouncy-bouncy, flirty hemlines with plenty of interest. It's all good fun, and you can have as much fun as you want!

Bottom up

Bottom up requires more advance planning than top down. You need to decide about the bottom circumference of the skirt before you cast on, and you have to know exactly what your hemline is going to look like—there is no opportunity to adjust or play around with it once you are halfway up the skirt. You have to decide how you will do the decreasing, if any, between hemline and hip. You also need to know the approximate finished length of the skirt, and when to begin the decreases at the hip, usually about 7" below the top of the skirt.

It's a little trickier to try on a bottom-up skirt while it's in process, but it can be done! Enlist someone to help you hold the skirt up while you try it on.

If you are unsure about yarn amounts, this blueprint could prove stressful. Look for a skirt pattern with a similar silhouette and yarn weight to what you desire, then purchase an equivalent amount of yarn plus a bit more—any extra can always be used for a matching accessory.

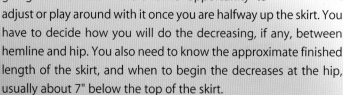

When deciding whether to work top to bottom or bottom to top, one consideration is the stitch pattern. Cast on and knit, say, four 8-row repeats. Look at the swatch, holding it with the cast-on at the top (the waist), then at the bottom (the hemline). If it looks best with the cast-on at the hemline, you'll want to make a bottom-up skirt. (See the skirts on pages 90 and 94. Incidentally, they also highlight another way to add a bit of shape — by scaling a motif.)

Side to side

Always a treat to knit, side-to-side construction has some distinct advantages over its top-down and bottom-up cousins. The cast-on determines the length of the skirt; to make it shorter, just cast on fewer stitches. It is easy to mark your progress; hold it up to your waist and when it goes around you, it is finished!

Probably one of the main advantages of side-to-side construction is that vertical stripes — whether of color or texture — can be easily achieved without working several colors or several stitch patterns on the same row. (There's a little irony here, because one of the two intarsia projects in this book is *My Flock of Sheep Skirt* on page 82, and it is worked from side to side.)

This construction also leaves a window open for picking up at the hemline and making a horizontally constructed addition, as well as for picking up at the top of the skirt for a waistband or yoke. Combining horizontal and vertical knitting in one garment can add flattering geometric interest.

This skirt's rate of increase is a bit more tricky. Rather than the conventional, easy way of increasing in a top-down skirt or decreasing in a bottom-up construction, a side-to-side skirt is shaped with short rows. In order to knit a skirt that is narrower at the waist and wider at the hemline, more rows need to be worked at the bottom, fewer rows at the top. A series of wedges (gores) fit together to make that A-line shape. While it is really just easy math, I think it is best to plan this shaping out on a schematic before beginning, as this direction of knitting accommodates fewer changes once it's on the needles.

Components of a side-to-side skirt

If you like shaping with short rows, this construction is perhaps the easiest to make smaller or larger. For a smaller skirt, decrease the number of gores, or work fewer pairs of full rows within each gore. For a larger skirt, add pairs of rows to each gore, or increase the number of gores.

Note that if you have a 6-gore skirt and add a pair of rows to each gore, your skirt will be 12 rows bigger at the waist, hip, and hemline. Each gore then tapers from, say, 5" at the waist, to 7" at the hip, to 10" at the hemline. While this may be what you need at the hip and waist, the bottom circumference might be out of hand.

To make the skirt longer or shorter, cast on more or fewer stitches, and adjust the number of stitches to be worked in each pair of short rows.

My Sideways Glance Skirt

Our back-cover skirt (also on page 74) has a 22-stitch stockinette yoke at the waist. The gores are shaped with 5 short-row pairs, each pair worked over 26 fewer stitches than the previous one. Instead, if you work 5 or 6 fewer stitches each time, adding one more short-row pair to the sequence, the bottom of the skirt will be wider.

To make the skirt longer, cast on 26 more stitches, adding one more short-row pair to the sequence. This would increase the length of the skirt by nearly 5".

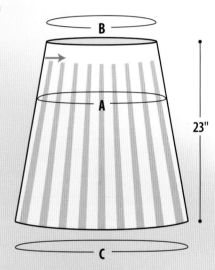

While there are other options such as modular construction (see *My Look at it from All Angles Skirt*, pages 110–115), these three choices should keep you in the successful skirt-knitting zone for the rest of your life.

...AND 4 MEASUREMENTS

What happens between the waist and hip is about you — *your fit*.

What happens below the hips is about the shape of the skirt, and your preference for length, fullness, and detail — *your style*.

YOUR FIT

Two measurements are needed for the fit of a pull-on skirt, allowing you to both pull it on and keep it in place: the waist and the hip.

Begin by locating *your waist*: it is where your body folds as you bend to the side. Tie a piece of yarn around your waist Now measure your waist, but do not pull the tape measure tight. Having zero ease would mean a skirt knit to the exact measurement of the waist, but our patterns allow more ease because these pull-on skirts need to slide over the hip, too. And because we are using elastic or a drawstring at the waist, the measurement needn't be exact.

Your hip can be a little more difficult to locate. Everyone's widest part falls at a different place, so *where this measurement is* — how many inches down from the waist — *is as important as what it is*. We are looking for your largest circumference. If it is not clear where this is, take measurements at several places and choose the largest, usually 7"–10" below the yarn tied at your waist; note this distance.

The hip is the A measurement on our schematics, and is the measurement we suggest you use when selecting the size to make. Note how far below the waist the pattern's A measurement was taken. Compare this to *the distance between your waist and hip* — you want to achieve your hip circumference within that distance, and doing so an inch or two higher than the hip is a sure way to guarantee a bit of ease at the hip — and that's a good thing. We want our skirts to flow from our waist over our hips and thighs without restriction.

A skirt could be a straight tube. If that tube was large enough to fit over the hips easily though, it would need to gather in quite a bit at the waist. That means lots of bulk — not attractive and probably not comfortable — so we eliminate the bulk by adding shaping. The most important shaping happens between the waist and the hip. A skirt should fit smoothly around the waist, then glide over the hips with little or no resistance.

IN BRIEF

1 Measure yourself.
2 Choose a skirt size based on your hip measurement.
3 Check the waist measurement of that size.
   • Modify if necessary.
4 Check the length between waist and hips.
   • Modify if necessary.
5 Check the skirt's total length.
   • Modify if you wish.
5 Check the skirt's bottom circumference
   • Modify if you wish.

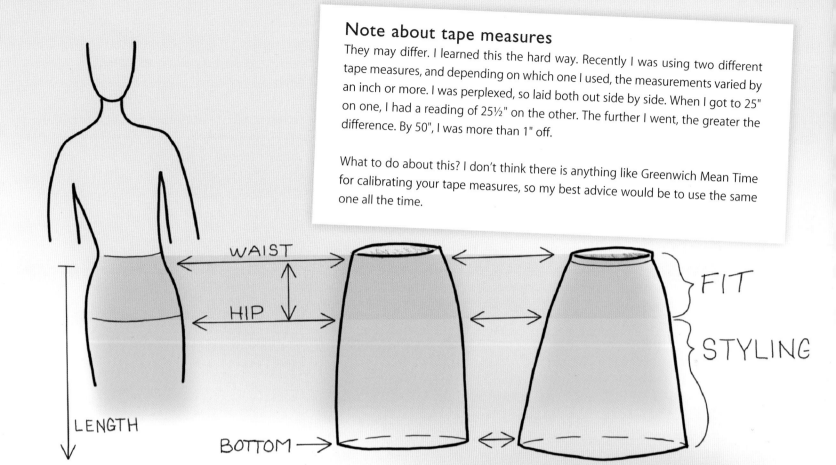

Note about tape measures
They may differ. I learned this the hard way. Recently I was using two different tape measures, and depending on which one I used, the measurements varied by an inch or more. I was perplexed, so laid both out side by side. When I got to 25" on one, I had a reading of 25½" on the other. The further I went, the greater the difference. By 50", I was more than 1" off.

What to do about this? I don't think there is anything like Greenwich Mean Time for calibrating your tape measures, so my best advice would be to use the same one all the time.

WAIST

HIP

LENGTH

BOTTOM →

FIT

STYLING

YOUR STYLE

Once you've developed a plan for fit, it's time for the styling, and that means we need more measurements: the length and the bottom circumference..

Length

As crucial as length can be, it really is a personal aesthetic; you know what you like and what you'll wear. If not…shopping expedition.

Love it or not, shopping is a great opportunity to evaluate what works for you—3-way mirrors and multiple sizes and lengths help you narrow the field to fit your target.

Length is usually about rows or rounds per inch. Those rounds aren't worked independently—they work in tandem with shaping the desired silhouette to arrive at the full bottom circumference.

Bottom circumference

This is the finished measurement located at the bottom edge of your skirt, and is mostly a consideration of style.

The smaller the bottom circumference, the less knitting you have to do. A narrow silhouette (think pencil skirt) or a very long silhouette can limit the length of your stride and hinder movement.

Our schematics do not usually give the circumference at the very bottom. Instead our measurement is usually taken after the last increase round (or before the first decrease round of a bottom-up skirt). Often the bottom circumference will actually be slightly larger than that. Seems illogical, but Rick Mondragon explains it as the result of hung gauge (see page 19).

Shaping a skirt

For most skirts the waist circumference is smaller than the hip, and the hip is smaller than the bottom.

When knitting from the top down, shaping involves increases; from the bottom up, it calls for decreases, and with side-to-side construction, it uses wedges — called gores — created by short-row shaping.

Much of a skirt's design is determined by where the shaping is placed. Most skirts are divided into 4 to 8 sections (usually called panels) — and stack increases vertically. This reflects what happens in a woven skirt's darts, or in shaped gores. These increases could be placed within a panel or between panels, individually or in pairs.

For example, a skirt with 6 panels might contain an increase or decrease in the middle of each panel, which would result in 6 more or 6 fewer stitches per shaping round. Or you might want to increase or decrease on each side of each panel, which would result in a difference of 12 stitches per shaping round.

Rate of increase or decrease

Let's focus on top-down construction (For bottom-up construction, reverse the direction of the shaping and replace increases with decreases.)

The **rate** refers to how much and how often you are going to increase, over how many rounds. It defines the shape of the skirt.

As we view our options, let's divide the silhouette into a waist-to-hip section and a hip-to-bottom section.

Steady rate Increases are worked from the waist to the desired hip size, then continue at the same rate to the hemline. The result is an A-line or conical shape.

You increase **x** stitches every **y** rounds for the entire length of the skirt.

Uneven rate After increases are made to the desired hip size, the increasing is slowed (more rounds between the increase rounds), continuing all plain or part of the way to the hemline for more of a dirndl shape with the benefit of no gathers. The rate of increase can continue to graduate. Especially with a longer skirt, this can be very useful in maintaining the shape without making the hemline too wide.

There are two other ways to increase at an uneven rate:

Increase to hip, then stop Increases are made to desired hip size, then stopped for a pencil skirt.

Increase to hip, then speed up Increases are made to the desired hip size, then fewer plain rounds are worked between the increase rounds as you head beyond for anything from a trumpet to an almost-full-circle silhouette.

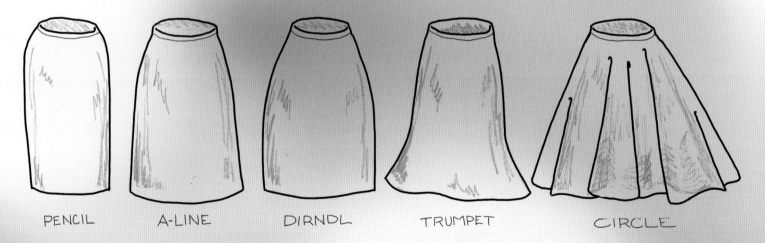

PENCIL   A-LINE   DIRNDL   TRUMPET   CIRCLE

For circumference (and thus shape), it doesn't really matter where the increases are done; the average rate (number of stitches over number of rounds) determines the shape of the piece.

To slow down the rate:

Work fewer increases.

OR

Work the same number of increases farther apart — more plain rounds between increase rounds.

To speed up the rate:

Work more increases.

OR

Work the same number of increases closer together — fewer plain rounds between increase rounds.

Applying this:

When the increases stack vertically, a dart or shaped panel becomes a visible design feature. To adjust the shaping rate for this style while maintaining the look, adjust the frequency of the increase rounds — skipping or adding increases within a round would be too noticeable.

In other cases, adjusting the number of increases within an increase round may be the most flexible method.

An uneven rate.

A steady rate.

If I hadn't knit a skirt before, I would probably choose one of the basic 4- or 6-gore, top-down patterns. I suggest you do so as well!

- First, compare the measurements of a similar skirt silhouette from your closet, or go to the mall and find one to use for comparison.
- Check body measurements, then pick a size.
  Is there anything you need to modify?
- Knit a nice big swatch (at least 6"–8" square), steam it, wash it, then take all those handy measurements.
- Start knitting.
- After 2"–3", spread the stitches out on 2 or 3 circulars, add point protection for security (don't want any stitches falling off), and slip it on — over tights, a body shaper, a slip, or whatever you plan to wear under it.)
- Check it out in a full-length mirror.
- Don't stress at this point; when finished, the skirt will definitely look better than it does now. Just confirm that it is working out. It's not a bad idea to hang it on a skirt hanger, steam it, and let it dry *before* you try it on.
- Continue to try it on every couple of inches, at least to the hip, then another time or two before the bind-off, to check the length and fullness.
- When you know the process is going well, you might want to stop and add elastic, a drawstring, or a repurposed top. That will make those try-on sessions less awkward and offer an even more realistic preview.

The top-down skirt is a personal favorite of mine, for many reasons. I have found that I can change my mind about many design aspects of the skirt while right in the middle of the knitting. Getting a waist measurement and casting on the stitches are the first steps. From there, a decision needs to be made about the rate of increase. Once the hip measurement is reached, you are pretty much free to do whatever you want for the rest of the skirt, such as adding embellishments, changing colors, changing stitch patterns, etc. You can continue increasing at the same rate or at a different rate, or do no further increasing at all.

Usually I find myself thinking about doing something different at the hem than what I had originally planned. This is all good fun, and you can have as much fun as you want! I love flouncy-bouncy, flirty hemlines with all kinds of interest. All you need to do is knit until it's the desired length—a number sometimes determined by the amount of yarn available!

Top down makes it easy to try on as you go—just put your stitches onto 2 circular needles, or onto a thread. I think it's important to try the skirt on every few inches until you're sure it's what you want. I know you know this already, but it is less stressful to rip out 2 inches than 6 inches!

top down

my Little Black Skirt

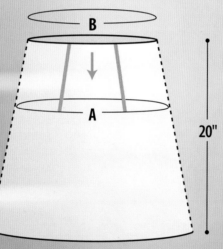

A 37 (38, **40½**, 42½, **44½**, 47½, **50**, 53)"
*approximately 7" below waist, after last
increase round*

B 25½ (27, 29, 31, **33**, 36, **38½**, 41½)"

gauge

25 stitches

32 rounds

in 10cm/4"
over stockinette
stitch, using MC

needles

3.75mm/US5, or size to
obtain gauge, 60cm/24"
or longer

notions

stitch markers

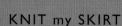
¾" elastic to
fit waist

shaping

4 darts Inc 2 at each dart every 6 rounds 9 times.
Shaping ends approximately 7" below the waist.

KNIT my SKIRT

What could be more classic than a little black skirt? Add a hint of bright pink stainless steel detail at the hemline for this not-so-classic version.

The first few rows of the waist are worked in a dropped-stitch pattern—an easy way to make a casing for elastic, and no double thickness!

yarn

 light weight
3 MC 600 (625, **675**, 700, **750**, 800, **850**, 900) yds

 lace weight
0 CC 145 (150, **160**, 170, **180**, 190, **200**, 215) yds

Shown in Size 38: LION BRAND LB Collection Superwash Merino in color 153 Night Sky (MC) and LION BRAND LB Collection Wool Stainless Steel in color 195 Azalea (CC)

WAISTBAND

With MC, cast on **158** (170, **182**, 194, **206**, 224, **242**, 260). Place marker (pm) and join to work in the round, being careful not to twist stitches.

Use a marker of a different color here.

Round 1 Knit.

Round 2: Elongate stitches **[K1, yo 3 times]** to end.

Round 3 Knit, dropping all yos.

BODY

Next round: Place markers for dart placement **[Knit 1/6 stitches, pm, k2, pm, knit 1/6 stitches, pm, k2, pm, knit 1/6 stitches]** twice.

Rounds 1–5 Knit.

Round 6: Increase round **[Knit to marker, M1L, slip marker (sm), k2, sm, M1R]** 4 times, knit to end — 8 stitches increased.

Work Rounds 1–6 a total of 9 times — **230** (242, **254**, 266, 278, 296, **314**, 332) stitches.

Work even in stockinette stitch until piece measures 15", or 5" less than desired length.

With CC, knit 8 rounds.

With MC, knit 5 rounds.

With CC, knit 3 rounds.

With MC, knit 5 rounds.

With CC, knit 8 rounds.

With MC, knit 13 rounds.

dart placement

1/6
1/6   1/6
— *beginning of round*
1/6   1/6
1/6

1/6 *stitches = k25*
*(27, **29**, 31, **33**, 36, **39**, 42) stitches*

HEM

With MC, purl 1 round; knit 5 rounds. Bind off loosely.

The last 5 rounds of stockinette stitch will roll up toward the purl round.

FINISHING

Cut elastic to desired length plus 1". Weave through elongated stitches at waistband; overlap and sew ends together.

notes

For any unfamiliar abbreviations and techniques, see page 116.

plan your own

Cast on a multiple of 6 + 2.

Subtract 8 dart stitches (2 stitches between markers at each of 4 darts) from the cast-on number, then divide by 6 for dart placement (1/6). Place markers as shown on diagram.

𝒱ariation

For truly classic black with no embellishments, leave out the stainless steel stripes at the bottom.

my not-so-classic skirt

How do you make My Little Black Skirt's cousin flirty? By adding a few more increase rounds and a ruffle at the hemline. This skirt's stainless steel bands are worked in garter stitch.

25

Shown in Size 33: BLUE SKY ALPACAS Skinny Cotton in color 321 Island Blue (MC) and NEIGHBORHOOD FIBER CO Chromium in color Belair (CC)

shaping
4 darts Inc 2 at each dart every 7 rounds, then every 10 rounds.

gauge

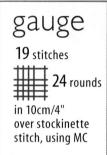

19 stitches

24 rounds

in 10cm/4" over stockinette stitch, using MC

needles

3.75mm/US5, or size to obtain gauge, 60cm/24" or longer

notions

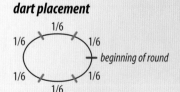

stitch markers

¾" elastic to fit waist

OR

2½" repurposed top

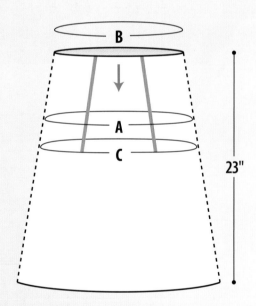

B 24½ (27, **29½**, 30½, **33½**, 36, **38½**, 42)"

A 33 (35½, **38**, 39, **41½**, 44, **46½**, 50½)"

C 38 (40½, **43**, 44, **46½**, 49½, **52**, 55½)"

23"

A 33 (35½, **38**, 39, **41½**, 44, **46½**, 50½)" *approximately 6" below waist, after 5 (3) increase rounds*

B 24½ (27, **29½**, 30½, **33½**, 36, **38½**, 42)" *approximately 2" more with repurposed top*

C 38 (40½, **43**, 44, **46½**, 49½, **52**, 55½)" *circumference after last increase round*

Length includes ruffle.

With MC, cast on **116** (128, **140**, 146, **158**, 170, **182**, 200); **132** (144, **156**, 162, **174**, 186, **198**, 216). Place marker (pm) and join to work in the round, being careful not to twist stitches.

Use a marker of a different color here.

Knit waistband

Work Rounds 1–3 of Waistband on page 24.

Place markers for dart placement: Set-up round **[Knit 1/6 stitches, pm, k2, pm, knit 1/6 stitches, pm, k2, pm, knit 1/6 stitches]** twice.

Rounds 1–6 Knit.

Round 7: Increase round [Knit to marker, M1L, slip marker (sm), k2, sm, M1R] 4 times, knit to end—8 stitches increased.

dart placement

1/6   1/6
1/6   1/6   — beginning of round
1/6   1/6

*1/6 stitches = k18 (20, **22**, 23, **25**, 27, **29**, 32); 20 (22, **24**, 25, **27**, 31, **34**) stitches*

Work Rounds 1–7 a total of 5 (3) times, then work Increase Round every 10 rounds 3 more times—**180** (192, **204**, 210, **222**, 234, **246**, 264) stitches. Knit 10 rounds.

Remove all markers except beginning-of-round marker. Work even until piece measures 18", or 5" less than desired length including ruffle.

yarn

light weight
MC 500 (550, **575**, 600, **650**, 675, **725**, 775) yds
allow 5% less if using repurposed top

lace weight
CC 225 (250, **260**, 270, **285**, 305, **325**, 350) yds

notes

1 For unfamiliar abbreviations and techniques, see page 116.
2 For KNIT WAISTBAND, use black numbers throughout AND do not work Repurposed Top.
3 For REPURPOSED TOP, use blue numbers if given, black numbers if not, AND do not work Knit Waistband.

Hem

With MC, knit 4 rounds.
With CC, knit 1 round; purl 3 rounds; knit 1 round.
With MC, knit 3 rounds.
With CC, knit 1 round; purl 6 rounds; knit 1 round.
With MC, knit 3 rounds; purl 1 round.
With MC, bind off all stitches in purl.

Ruffle

With RS of skirt facing, fold back the hem so you are looking at the WS. Find the last round that has both MC and CC bumps (see illustration *1*). With CC, pick up and knit into each of the CC bumps from that round (see *2a* and *2b*) — **180** (192, **204**, 210, **222**, 234, **246**, 264) stitches. Pm and join to work in the round. Do not turn work. Knit 3 rounds.

Next round: Increase round **[K3 (3, 3, 3, 4, 4, 4, 4), yo]**, repeat to last k**0** (0, **0**, 0, **2**, 2, **2**, 0) stitches — **60** (64, **68**, 70, **55**, 58, **61**, 66) stitches increased; **240** (256, **272**, 280, **276**, 292, **304**, 328) total stitches.

Next round: Adjust stitch count Knit, knitting through the back loop of each yo from the previous round AND adjusting stitch count to a multiple of 4 by decreasing **0** (0, **0**, 0, **1**, 0, **3**, 2) — **240** (256, **272**, 280, **277**, 292, **307**, 330) stitches.

Increase every other round as follows, working the yos tbl on the plain rounds.
Round 1 **[K4, yo]** to end.
Rounds 2, 4, 6, 8, and 10 Knit.

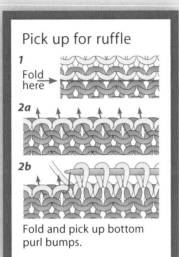

Pick up for ruffle

1
Fold here →

2a

2b

Fold and pick up bottom purl bumps.

Round 3 **[K5, yo]** to end.
Round 5 **[K6, yo]** to end.
Round 7 **[K7, yo]** to end.
Round 9 **[K8, yo]** to end.
Round 11 **[Kf&b]** to end.
Round 12 Knit.
Bind off.

FINISHING

For knit waistband, finish as on page 24.
OR
See page 8 to attach repurposed top to skirt.

plan your own

Cast on a multiple of 6 + 2.
Subtract 8 dart stitches (2 stitches between markers at each of 4 darts) from the cast-on number, then divide by 6 for dart placement (1/6).
Place markers as shown on diagram:

variations

V1 · Don't like ruffles? Just make a stockinette-stitch or garter-stitch underlay. Pick up as for ruffle.
V2 · Make more stainless steel stripes at bottom; alter the widths.

my

this chick
means Business

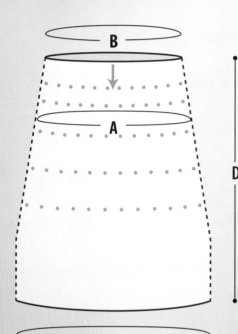

shaping
- Increase 1 stitch in purl section of each repeat 5 times.

A 34 (37, **40**, 43, **47**)"
approximately 6" below waist, after second increase round; slightly stretched

B 28½ (30½, **32½**, 34½, **36½**)"
approximately 1½" more at top of knit piece for repurposed top; slightly stretched

C 65 (67½, **69½**, 72, **74½**)"
after last increase round

D 24"
approximately 2½" longer with repurposed top

needles

3.5mm/US4, or size to obtain gauge, 60cm/24" or longer
AND
needle 2–3 sizes smaller for knit waistband

notions

¼" elastic to fit waist
OR
3" repurposed top

gauge

28 stitches

42 rounds

in 10cm/4" worked in Slip Stitch Rib over 7 stitches

KNIT my SKIRT

A classically designed skirt with the subtle lure of pseudo pleats, this skirt drapes like a charm from the heavenly combination of fiber in the yarn. The pleats widen out ever so slightly as they travel to the hem, then do an about-face and fill in. The hem is finished off in the most beautiful way ever… a tubular bind-off.

yarn

  fine weight
1675 (1800, **1950**, 2075, **2225**) yds

Shown in Size 34: HIKOO CoBaSi in color Raffi

notes

1 For unfamiliar abbreviations and techniques, see page 116.
2 Change to longer needle as stitches are increased.

Sl 1

Slip stitch purlwise with yarn at WS of work.

Slip Rib

Round 1 [**K1, purl to k rib**] to end.
Round 2 [**Sl 1, purl to k rib**] to end.
Repeat Rounds 1 and 2.

variations

To me, this skirt, offered in a huge range of sizes, is the perfect mathematical equation of aesthetic beauty. To change any of the ratios of the sections might be treason, but of course there are options:

V1 · If you don't care for the k1, p1 rib at the very bottom of the skirt, you can continue with the established pattern of the wider rib. The only caveat: you won't be able to use the tubular bind-off.

V2 · If you don't want to split the ribs toward the bottom, you can continue increasing in each purl section instead.

SKIRT

With larger needle, loop cast on **171** (177, **183**, 189, **195**).

Knit waistband

With smaller needle, knit 1 row; purl 1 row.
Next row: Eyelet row K1, [**k2tog, yo**] to last stitch, k1. Purl 1 row; knit 1 row. Continuing with smaller needle, work as directed through Increase Round 1, then change to larger needle.

Repurposed top

Continuing with larger needle, knit 1 row; purl 1 row; knit 1 row.

Place marker (pm) and join to work in the round, being careful not to twist stitches.
Round 1: Begin Slip Rib [**K1, p2**] to end.
Round 2 [**Sl 1, p2**] to end.
Repeat Rounds 1 and 2 eight more times.

Increase round 1 [**K1, p1, M1P, p1**] to end — **57** (59, **61**, 63, **65**) stitches increased on this and every increase round. ***Next round*** [**Sl 1, p3**] to end.
Next 18 rounds Work even in Slip Rib as established.

M1P

Insert left needle from front to back under strand between last stitch worked and first stitch on left needle. Purl, twisting strand by working into loop at back of needle from left to right.

Completed: a left-slanting increase.

Increase round 2 **[K1, p2, M1P, p1]** to end.
Next round **[Sl 1, p4]** to end.
Next 18 rounds Work even in Slip Rib as established.

Increase round 3 **[K1, p2, M1P, p2]** to end.
Next round **[Sl 1, p5]** to end.
Next 18 rounds Work even in Slip Rib as established.

Increase round 4 **[K1, p3, M1P, p2]** to end.
Next round **[Sl 1, p6]** to end.
Next 36 rounds Work even in Slip Rib as established.

Increase round 5 **[K1, p3, M1P, p3]** to end.
Next round **[Sl 1, p7]** to end.
Next 36 rounds Work even in Slip Rib as established.

Next round: Divide the rib repeats **[K1, p3]** to end.
Next round **[Sl 1, p3]** to end.
Work even in Slip Rib as established for 34 rounds, or
until piece measures 3" less than desired length.

Next round: Divide the rib repeats **[K1, p1]** to end.
Next round **[Sl 1, p1]** to end.
Work 29 rounds even in established rib.
Bind off all stitches using tubular bind-off.

FINISHING

Sew first few rows together at waist.
Cut elastic to desired length plus 1". Weave
through eyelets at knit waistband; overlap and sew
ends together.
OR
See page 8 to attach repurposed top to skirt.

my la Bohème *skirt*

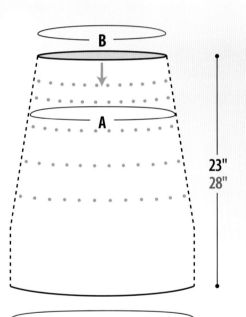

A 39 (45, **50**)"
39 (46, **53**)"
*approximately 5–6" below
waist, after 4 increase rounds*

B 28 (33½, **36½**)"
30 (33, **36**)"

C 74–80"
*approximate circumference
after last increase round*

23"
28"

gauge

20 (**17**) stitches
32 rounds
(**26**) rounds
in 10cm/4"
over stockinette
stitch, washed
and dried

needles

3.75mm/US5, or size to
obtain gauge, 60cm/24"
AND longer

notions

stitch markers

¼" elastic to
fit waist

shaping
- **14 repeats of Slip Rib around skirt**
- Increase 1 stitch in purl section
of every repeat 12 times.

While using the same stitch
pattern as *My This Chick Means
Business Skirt*, this sister is a bit
more Bohemian. Long or short,
it is definitely a skirt to play the
cello in! Elastic makes the waist
comfortable — size it up or down.

yarn

light weight
3
short version: **925** (1000,
1050, 1150, **1225**) yds

long version: **1050** (1125,
1200, 1300, **1350**) yds

Shown in Size 39:
Short version: SCHOPPEL WOLLE
Leinen Los in color 9093
SchwarzMélange

Long version: TWISTED SISTERS
Essential in color 87 Handpaint

MY Concerto SKIRT

With a swing and a drape, this skirt has a surprise at the hemline — stripes! An elastic eyelet waistband ensures a comfortable fit.

gauge

23 stitches

28 rounds

in 10cm/4" over stockinette stitch, after washing and drying

notions

stitch markers

¾" elastic to fit waist
OR
3" repurposed top

needles

3.75mm/US5
or size to obtain gauge, 60cm/24" or longer

A 38 (40½, **43½**, 45, **46½**, 49½, **51**, 54, **55½**)"
approximately 5" below waist, before third increase round

B 30½ (33½, **36**, 37½, **39**, 41½, **43**, 46, **47½**)"
approximately 2½" more with repurposed top

C 64 (67, **67**, 68½, **70**, 70, **71½**, 71½, **72½**)"
circumference after last increase round

shaping

16 panels alternating panels of stockinette stitch (knit every round) and reverse stockinette stitch (purl every round). Increases are made on each side of each purl panel, 16 stitches every 12 rounds.

yarn

fine weight

2

MC 750 (800, **850**, 875, **900**, 925,
950, 975, **1000**) yds
allow 5% less if using repurposed top

A 25 (30, **30**, 30, **30**, 35, **35**, 35,
35) yds

B 95 (100, **110**, 110, **115**, 120, **120**,
125, **130**) yds

Shown in Size 38: LOUET NORTH AMERICA
Euroflax Sport Weight Linen in colors Steel
Gray (MC), Eggplant (A), and Rose (B)

With MC, loop cast on **176** (192, **208**, 216, **224**, 240, **248**, 264, **272**) 192 (208, **224**, 232, **240**, 256, **264**, 280, **288**). Place marker (pm) and join to work in the round, being careful not to twist stitches.

Use a marker of a different color here.

Knit waistband
Round 1 Knit.
Round 2: Elongate stitches **[K1, yo 3 times]** to end of round.
Round 3 Knit, dropping all yos from previous round.

Repurposed top
Knit 3 rounds.

BODY
Next round: Place panel markers **[K21 (23, 25, 26, 27, 29, 30, 32, 33), pm, p1 (3), pm]** to end.
No need to place last marker, it is beginning-of-round marker.
Work 11 rounds in established knit/purl pattern.
Next round: Increase round **[Knit to marker, slip marker (sm), yo, purl to marker, yo, sm]** to end — 16 stitches increased.
Next 11 rounds Work in established knit/purl pattern, purling through the back loop of each yo on the first round.
Work last 12 rounds **10** (10, **9**, 9, **9**, 8, **8**, 7, **7**); **9** (9, **8**, 8, **8**, 7, **7**, 6, **6**) more times — **23** (23, **21**, 21, **21**, 19, **19**, 17, **17**) stitches in each reverse-stockinette-stitch section — **352** (368, **368**, 376, **384**, 384, **392**, 392, 400) stitches. Work even until piece measures 18" (15"), or 3" (6") from desired length.

Striped border
Next round Purl, removing all markers except beginning-of-round marker.
Knit 20 rounds as follows: 2 rounds A, 2 rounds B, 3 rounds A, 3 rounds B, 5 rounds A, 5 rounds B. Purl 1 round B. Bind off very loosely.

FINISHING
Cut elastic to desired length plus 1". Weave through elongated stitches at knit waistband; overlap and sew ends together.
OR
See page 8 to attach repurposed top to skirt.
Machine wash and dry.

See page 8 to attach repurposed top to skirt.

notes
1 *For unfamiliar abbreviations and techniques, see page 116.*
2 *For KNIT WAISTBAND, use black numbers throughout AND do not work Repurposed Top.*
3 *For REPURPOSED TOP, use blue numbers if given, black numbers if not, AND do not work Knit Waistband.*

my square root skirt

A skirt knit in linen using linen stitch = linen squared.

Divide the bottom of this skirt and insert 8 little diamonds, and you've got instant hem attraction. A purchased waistband makes a sleek 3" top.

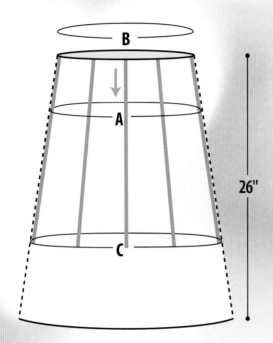

A 38 (41, **43½**, 46, **49**, 51)
approximately 5½" below waist, after second increase round

B 30 (32½, **35½**, 38, **41**, 43½)
approximately 2½" more with repurposed top

C 43½ (46½, **49**, 49, **51½**, 54½)"
circumference after last increase round

shaping

8 panels Increase at each edge of each panel — 16 stitches every 28 rounds.

gauge

23½ stitches

40 rounds

in 10cm/4"
over linen stitch,
after washing and
drying

notions

stitch markers

¾" elastic to fit
waist
OR
3" repurposed top

needles

3.5mm/US4, or size to
obtain gauge, 60cm/24"
or longer

yarn

2 **fine weight**
MC 950 (1025, **1075**, 1125, **1200**, 1300) yds

1 **super fine weight**
CC 50 yds (optional)

Shown in Size 41: CLAUDIA HAND PAINTED YARNS Drama in color Teal (MC) and Contemplation in color Charlotte's Verdigris (CC)

my Swirling Skirt

This attractively feminine skirt has six sections that swirl their way around and end in a pretty little petal hemline.

needles

2.75mm/US2, or size to obtain gauge, 60cm/24" or longer

gauge

23 stitches

32 rounds

in 10cm/4" over stockinette stitch, after washing and drying

child's 4 (6, **8**, 10, **12**)

A & B 19 (21, **23**, 25, **27**)"

C 33½ (36½, **39½**, 43, **46**)" *circumference after last increase round*

D 13½ (13½, **16**, 16, **18½**)"

E 3 (3, **4**, 4, **5**)"

Shown in Size 8: PRISM YARNS Euroflax Sport Weight Linen in color Zinnia

notions

stitch markers

¼" elastic to fit waist

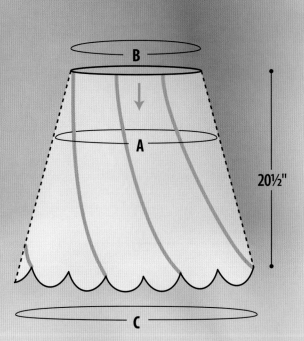

A 35 (37½, **39½**, 41½, **44**, 46, **48**, 50, **52**, 54½, **56½**)"
approximately 5" below waist, after 6 increase rounds

B 29 (31½, **33½**, 35½, **37½**, 39½, **41½**, 44, **46**, 48, **50**)"

C 56½ (58½, **60½**, 62½, **64½**, 67, **69**, 71, **73**, 75, **77**)"
circumference after last increase round

/ *shaping*

/ **6 panels** 3 stockinette-stitch panels; 3 Broken Rib panels.
Increase **6 stitches** every 6 rounds 24 times.

yarn

fine weight
adult 875 (925, **975**, 1025, **1100**, 1150, **1200**, 1250, **1300**, 1350, **1400**) yds
child 375 (425, **500**, 550, **675**) yds

Shown in Size 35: PRISM YARNS Euroflax Sport Weight Linen in color Honeydew

SKIRT

Cast on **108** (120, **132**, 144, **156**, **168**, 180, **192**, 204, **216**, 228, **240**, 252, **264**, 276, **288**).

Waistband

Knit 1 row; purl 1 row. *Next row: Eyelet row* K1, **[k2tog, yo]** to last stitch, k1. Purl 1 row; knit 1 row.

Place marker (pm) and join to work in the round, being careful not to twist stitches.

Begin patterns: Round 1 **[K16 (18, 20, 22, 24, 26, 28, 30, 32, 34, 36, 38, 40, 42, 44, 46), pm, k2 tbl, pm, work 16 (18, 20, 22, 24, 26, 28, 30, 32, 34, 36, 38, 40, 42, 44, 46) in Broken Rib, pm, k2 tbl, pm]** to end.

> *No need to place last marker, it is the beginning-of-round marker.*

Round 2 **[Knit to marker, k2 tbl between markers, work Broken Rib to marker, k2 tbl between markers]** to end.

CHILD'S SIZES ONLY: Repeat last round for **3** (3, **4**, 4, **5**)".

Begin shaping

Rounds 1, 3, and 5: LT round **[Knit to marker, remove marker (rm), k1, place marker back onto right needle, sl 1 purlwise, rm from left needle, slip stitch back to left needle, work LT, pm back on right needle, work in Broken Rib to marker, rm, work next stitch into existing rib stitch, pm back onto right needle, sl 1 purlwise, rm from left needle, slip stitch back to left needle, work LT, pm back on right needle]** to end.

> *Beginning-of-round marker will now be 1 stitch farther to the left than in previous round.*

Round 2: Increase round **[Work to marker, M1L, k2 tbl]** to end — 6 stitches increased.

Rounds 4 and 6 **[Work to marker, k2 tbl]** to end.

Work Rounds 1–6 a total of **14** (14, **16**, 16, **18**) times for child's sizes; 26 times for woman's sizes, then work Round 1 once more for all sizes — **30** (32, **36**, 38, **42**, **52**, 54, **56**, 58, **60**, 62, **64**, 66, **68**, 70, **72**) stitches in each section.

> *Adjust length here if desired. You can make your skirt longer by repeating the 6 rounds WITHOUT increases, working Round 2 the same as Rounds 4 and 6. Every 6 rounds add approximately 1" to the length.*

Remove all markers except beginning-of-round marker.

plan your own

Cast on a multiple of 12.

variations

V1 · Substitute any stitch pattern for the Broken Rib sections, working the increases into that pattern.

V2 · Instead of making two petals for the hemline in every section, make one petal per section.

notes

1 For unfamiliar abbreviations and techniques, see page 116.

2 Skirt is knit from the top down on a circular needle. There are 6 panels in the skirt, alternating between stockinette stitch and Broken Rib. Panels are separated by a left twist which moves 1 stitch to the left every other round.

3 The first 5 numbers shown in green are for child sizes; the last 11 numbers, shown in black, are for adult sizes.

LT (LEFT TWIST)

Round 1 Skip 1 stitch, knit into the back of the second stitch, then knit through the backs of both stitches together and slip from the left needle.

Round 2 Knit through the back loops of both stitches, one at a time.

Broken Rib

over an even number of stitches

Round 1 [K1, p1] to end.

Round 2 Knit.

Repeat these 2 rounds, always working purl stitches above previous purl stitches.

K2 tbl

Knit through the back loop of the next 2 stitches, one at a time.

Petal Hemline

Each of the 12 petals is worked separately back and forth.

Purl 1 round, placing a marker every **16** (17, **19**, 20, **22**, **27**, 28, **29**, 30, **31**, 32, **33**, 34, **35**, 36, **37**) stitches.

Begin Petal short rows: SR 1 (RS) Knit to 1 stitch before marker, turn.

SR 2 (WS) Yo, knit to 1 stitch before marker, turn.

SR 3 Yo, k13 (14, **16**, 17, **19**, **24**, 25, **26**, 27, **28**, 29, **30**, 31, **32**, 33, **34**), turn.

SR 4 Yo, k12 (13, **15**, 16, **18**, **23**, 24, **25**, 26, **27**, 28, **29**, 30, **31**, 32, **33**), turn.

Continue as established, knitting 1 fewer stitch each row; end after a WS row of yo, k4 (3, **3**, 4, **4**, **3**, 4, **3**, 4, **3**, 4, **3**, 4, **3**). Turn.

Partial RS row Yo, knit to first yo on left needle, **[k2tog (yo together with next stitch)]** along edge of petal to marker.

Next WS row Knit to first yo, **[SSK, (yo together with next stitch)]** along edge of petal to marker.

Bind-off row K1, **[k1, insert left needle into front of 2 stitches on right needle and knit them together]** to marker, remove marker, bind off 1 — remaining stitch on right needle is first stitch of SR 1 of next petal.

Repeat for 11 more petals, beginning with SR 1. Fasten off last stitch of last petal.

Finishing

Sew first few rows together at waist.

Cut elastic to desired length plus 1". Weave through eyelets at knit waistband; overlap and sew ends together.

Machine wash and dry.

Petal

— Knit
— K2tog (yo and next stitch)
— SSK (yo and next stitch)
— Bind off
⊃ Turn and yo

Petal bind-off

1 Knit 1. *2* Knit 1 from left needle. *3* Insert Left needle into pair on right needle as shown.

4 Knit these 2 stitches together.
Repeat Steps 2–4.

my mummy skirt

Reminiscent of the linen wrappings on Egyptian mummies, the sections of this skirt swirl round and round. The stitch pattern is easily memorized, and you will be mesmerized in no time as you knit round and round. A repurposed top ensures a smooth waistline.

4½"

25"

☐ *repurposed top*

A 40½ (45, **49½**, 54, **58**)"
36 (39½, **43½**, 47½, **51**)"
approximately 2" below top of knit portion of skirt, after 4 repeats of pattern

B 35 (39½, **43½**, 48, **52½**)"
30½ (34½, **38½**, 42, **46**)"
top of knit portion of skirt

C 99 (103½, **107½**, 112, **116½**)"
87 (91, **94½**, 98½, **102½**)"
circumference after last increase round

black numbers show measurements BEFORE washing and drying, blue numbers AFTER washing and drying

gauge

22 (25) stitches
29 rounds
(35) rounds

in 10cm/4" over stockinette stitch, before (after) washing and drying (see note 2, page 50)

needles

3.5mm/US4, or size to obtain gauge, 60cm/24" AND longer

notions

stitch markers

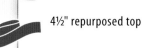
4½" repurposed top

shaping
8 sections in skirt 1 stitch increased each 4-round repeat of pattern

yarn

light weight
3 **1300** (1475, **1650**, 1825,
2000) yds

Shown in Size 36: KOLLAGE YARNS
Riveting Sport in 7903 Night Demin

49

my Amoeba skirt

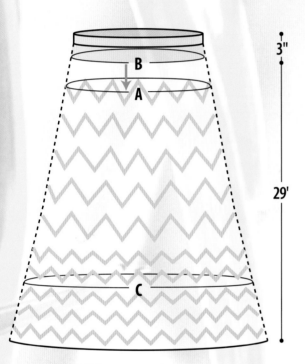

3"

29'

□ repurposed top

A 38 (41, **43½**, 46, **49**, 51½, **54**, 57)"
*approximately 4" below top of knit portion of skirt,
after second increase round*

B 28 (30, **32**, 34, **36**, 38, **40**, 42)"
top of knit portion of skirt

C 74 (79, **84**, 89, **95**, 100, **105**, 110)"
circumference before last increase round

 shaping

2 stitches increased in each repeat of ripple pattern
by working the increases but not the decreases.
When the 11-stitch ripples have been increased to
21 stitches, the 11-stitch repeat is worked again,
doubling the number of ripples (and the increases).

gauge

22 stitches

 28 rounds

in 10cm/4"
over stockinette
stitch

Each 11-stitch
repeat = 2" wide

needles

✗ **4mm/US6**, or size to
obtain gauge, 60cm/24"
AND longer

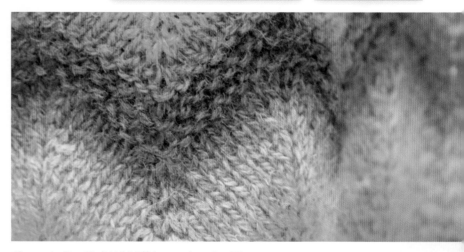

Shown in Size 33: KAUNI Effektgarn in color EZ

Waves of blurry color bands cascade down this lovely rippled skirt. Knit from the waist down, it has a purchased waistband, and the hem is graced with a gentle scallop.

notions

stitch markers

3" repurposed top

yarn

fine weight
2
1275 (1350, **1450**, 1550,
1650, 1725, **1825**, 1900) yds

53

my Green Valley skirt

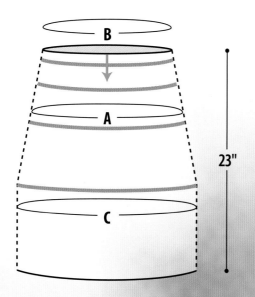

A 38 (42, **46**, 49½, **53**, 56½)"
measured in middle of Lacy Zigzag tier

B 30 (34, **37½**, 41, **44½**, 48)"

C 45½ (49, **55**, 59½, **63**, 66½)"

shaping
Increases are made in 4 eyelet ridges between tiers.

Can a rabbit inspire a skirt pattern? Evidently so! Rural Connecticut, where I live, has abundantly beautiful green valleys and fields. Each summer morning, along my bike ride, I stop at a different field to pick greens for my rabbit. Each edible plant has its own shade of green and its own unique leaf pattern.

needles

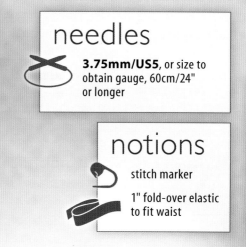

3.75mm/US5, or size to obtain gauge, 60cm/24" or longer

notions

stitch marker

1" fold-over elastic to fit waist

gauge

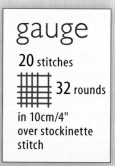

20 stitches

32 rounds

in 10cm/4" over stockinette stitch

yarn

super fine weight
1 **A and D** 125 (140, **155**, 165, **175**, 190) yds each
B 250 (275, **305**, 330, **355**, 375) yds
C 350 (385, **425**, 465, **500**, 525) yds

Shown in Size 38: GEILSK Cotton/Wool in colors C27 Spring Green (A), C3 Green (B), C36 Dark Army (C), and C16 Grey (D)

SKIRT

Work waist

Using loop cast-on and D, cast on **150** (168, **186**, 204, **222**, 240). Place marker and join to work in the round, being careful not to twist stitches. Work in stockinette stitch until piece measures 1½".

Work Eyelet Ridge

Change to A.

Round 1 Knit. *Round 2* Purl.

Round 3: Eyelet round **[Yo, k2tog]** to end.

Round 4: Increase P**12** (11, **9**, 8, **6**, 15), **[p6 (7, 8, 9, 10, 10), Inc 1]** 21 times, purl to end—**171** (189, **207**, 225, **243**, 261) stitches.

> *This and following increase rounds produce the multiples needed for the next tier's lace pattern.*

Work Zigzag Eyelets

Change to D and knit 1 round. Work Rounds 1–16 of Zigzag Eyelets.

Work Eyelet Ridge

Change to B.

Round 1 Knit to last 2 stitches, k2tog—**170** (188, **206**, 224, **242**, 260) stitches.

Round 2 Purl.

Round 3: Eyelet round **[Yo, k2tog]** to end.

Round 4: Increase P8 (6, **4**, 2, **0**, 9), **[p7 (8, 9, 10, 11, 11), Inc 1]** 22 times, purl to end—**192** (210, **228**, 246, **264**, 282) stitches.

Work Lacy Zigzag

Change to A and knit 1 round. Work Rounds 1–12 of Lacy Zigzag twice, then work Rounds 1–6 once more.

Work Eyelet Ridge

Change to C.

Round 1 Knit.

Round 2 Purl.

Round 3: Eyelet round **[Yo, k2tog]** to end.

Round 4: Increase P**12** (0, **9**, 18, **6**, 15), **[p4 (5, 5, 5, 6, 6), Inc 1]** 42 times, purl to end—**234** (252, **270**, 288, **306**, 324) stitches.

Work Fern Lace

Change to B and knit 1 round. Work Rounds 1–4 of Fern Lace 11 times.

Inc I

Loop cast on 1.

Stitch key

- ☐ *Knit*
- ⊙ *Yarn over (yo)*
- ◺ *SSK*
- ◿ *K2tog*
- *Right double decrease (RDD)*
- *Left double decrease (LDD)*
- → *Remove marker, sl 1 to left needle, replace marker*
- ← *Remove marker, sl 1 to right needle, replace marker*

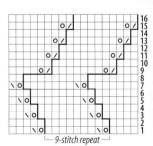

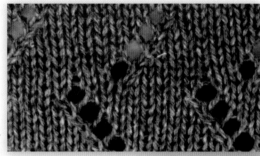

Zigzag Eyelets MULTIPLE OF 9

Round 1 K4, **[yo, SSK, k7]** to last 5 stitches, yo, SSK, k3.

Round 2 and every alternate round Knit.

Round 3 K5, **[yo, SSK, k7]** to last 4, yo, SSK, k2.

Round 5 K6, **[yo, SSK, k7]** to last 3, yo, SSK, k1.

Round 7 [K7, yo, SSK] to end.

Round 9 K3, **[k2tog, yo, k7]** to last 6, k2tog, yo, k4.

Round 11 K2, **[k2tog, yo, k7]** to last 7, k2tog, yo, k5.

Round 13 K1, **[k2tog, yo, k7]** to last 8, k2tog, yo, k6.

Round 15 **[K2tog, yo, k7]** to end.

Round 16 Knit.

Lacy Zigzag MULTIPLE OF 6

Round 1 Remove marker, sl 1 to left needle, replace marker, **[SSK, k2, yo, k2]** to end.

Round 2 and every alternate round Knit.

Rounds 3 and 5 **[SSK, k2, yo, k2]** to end.

Round 7 Remove marker, sl 1 to right needle, replace marker, **[k2, yo, k2, k2tog]** to end.

Rounds 9 and 11 **[K2, yo, k2, k2tog]** to end.

Round 12 Knit.

Work Eyelet Ridge

Change to D.

Round 1 Knit.

Rounds 2 and 4 Purl.

Round 3: Eyelet round **[Yo, k2tog]** to end.

Round 4: Increase P0 (0, **10**, 14, **18**, 22), **[p9 (9, 5, 5, 5, 5), Inc 1]** 26 (28, **50**, 52, **54**, 56) times, purl to end—**260** (280, **320**, 340, **360**, 380) stitches.

Work Staggered Fern Lace

Change to C and knit 1 round. Work Rounds 1–10 of Staggered Fern Lace 6 times.

Work hem

Rounds 1 and 3 Purl. *Round 2* **[Yo, k2tog]** to end.

Bind off all stitches as follows: **[K2tog through back loops, slip the stitch on the right needle to the left needle purlwise]** to end. Fasten off.

FINISHING

See page 10 to attach fold-over elastic to skirt.

note

For unfamiliar abbreviations and techniques, see page 116.

to adjust length

Add or eliminate rounds for the last 2 lace tiers.

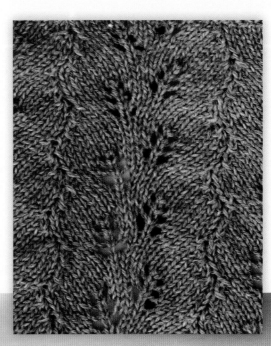

— 9-stitch repeat —

Fern Lace
MULTIPLE OF 9

Round 1 [K1, yo, k2, SSK, k2tog, k2, yo] to end.

Rounds 2 and 4 Knit.

Round 3 [Yo, k2, SSK, k2tog, k2, yo, k1] to end.

Staggered Fern Lace MULTIPLE OF 20

Right Double Decrease (RDD) K2tog, slip the stitch on the right needle to the left needle purlwise, pass second stitch on left needle over and off; slip remaining stitch to right needle purlwise.

Left Double Decrease (LDD) Slip 1 knitwise, k2tog, pass slipped stitch over and off needle.

Round 1 K11, yo, k1, yo, k5, LDD.

Round 2 and every alternate round Knit.

Round 3 K12, yo, k1, yo, k4, LDD.

Round 5 RDD, k6, yo, k1, yo, k3, yo, k1, yo, k3, LDD.

Round 7 RDD, k5, yo, k1, yo, k11.

Round 9 RDD, k4, yo, k1, yo, k12.

Round 10 Knit.

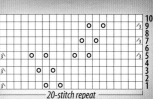
— 20-stitch repeat —

my Red velvet skirt

The lush colors of this easy slip-stitch pattern give the fabric a velvety surface that seems to have a nap when viewed from different angles.

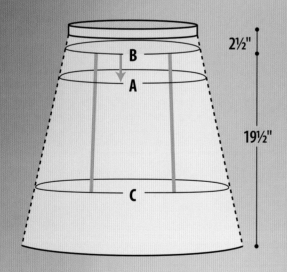

A 34 (37½, 40, 42½, 45½, 48, 50½)"
approximately 2" below top of knit portion of skirt, before second increase round

B 33½ (36, 38½, 41½, 44, 46½, 49½)"
top of knit portion

C 49½ (49½, 49½, 52, 54½, 57½, 60)"
circumference after last increase round

gauge

24 stitches

 **45** rounds

in 10cm/4"
over Slip Stitch Pattern

needles

3.75mm/US5, or size to obtain gauge, 60cm/24" or longer

notions

stitch markers

¼" elastic to fit waist
OR
3" repurposed top

shaping
4 panels Increase at beginning and end of each panel every 8 rounds: 8 times for red skirt; 14 times for blue skirt. For 2 smallest sizes, work additional increases as written.

yarn

light weight
3
MC 775 (825, **850**, 900, **950**, 1000, **1050**) yds
CC 425 (450, **475**, 500, **525**, 550, **575**) yds

Shown in Size 34: TRENDSETTER YARN
Merino VI in colors 7076 Dark Chocolate
(MC) and 8772 Burnt Rust (CC)

...and my Blue Rhapsody skirt

The shorter sister to Red Velvet, this skirt is the same shape and the same stitch pattern, and includes a knit waistband with a threaded elastic.

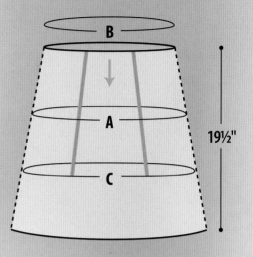

A 34 (37½, **40**, 42½, **45½**, 48, **50½**)" *approximately 5" below waist, after 7 increase rounds*

B 25½ (28, **30½**, 33½, **36**, 38½, **41½**)"

C 49½ (49½, **49½**, 52, **54½**, 57½, **60**)" *circumference after last increase round*

notes
1 For unfamiliar abbreviations and techniques, see page 116.
2 Work all increases as loop cast-on.
3 For KNIT WAISTBAND, use black numbers throughout.
4 For REPURPOSED TOP, use blue numbers if given, black numbers if not, AND do not work Knit Waistband.

Inc 1
Loop cast on 1 stitch.

Slip Stitch Pattern
Slip stitches purlwise with yarn at WS of work.
Rounds 1 and 2 With MC, knit.
Round 3 With CC, [(k1, sl 1) to 1 *before* marker, k1, slip marker (sm), sl 1, sm] to end.
Round 4 With CC, [(p1, sl 1) to 1 *before* marker, p1, sm, sl 1, sm] to end.

yarn

light weight
[3]
MC 750 (800, **825**, 875, **925**, 975, **1050**) yds
CC 400 (425, **450**, 475, **500**, 525, **550**) yds

Shown in Size 34: TRENDSETTER YARN Merino VI in colors 8964 Royal Blue (MC) and 6664 French Blue (CC)

With MC, cast on **152** (168, **184**, 200, **216**, 232, **248**); **200** (216, **232**, 248, **264**, 280, **296**). Knit 1 row; purl 1 row. Place marker (pm) and join to work in the round, being careful not to twist stitches.

Use a marker of a different color here.

Knit waistband

Round 1: Elongate stitches **[K1, yo 3 times]** to end of round.

Round 2 Knit, dropping all yos from previous round.

Knit 3 rounds.

BODY

Next round: Place markers for dart placement **[K37 (41, 45, 49, 53, 57, 61); 49 (53, 57, 61, 65, 69, 73), place marker (pm), k1]** to end.

No need to place last marker, it is the beginning-of-round marker.

Work 7 rounds in Slip Stitch Pattern.

Next round: Increase round **[Inc 1, work to marker, Inc 1, slip marker (sm), work stitch between markers, sm]** to end—8 stitches increased.

Continue in pattern, working Increase Round every 8 rounds 13 (7) more times, then **[work Increase Round every 24 rounds, then every 8 rounds]** 2 (1, **0**, 0, **0**, 0, **0**) times—**296** (296, **296**, 312, **328**, 344, **360**) stitches; **73** (73, **73**, 77, **81**, 85, **89**) stitches in each section (does not include single stitch between markers). Work even in pattern until piece measures 18½" (19"), end with Round 4.

Hem options: Red Velvet's seed hem gives a sleek finish; Blue Rhapsody's is twice as deep and flares a bit.

Seed hem

Rounds 1 and 2 With MC, knit.

Round 3 **[K1, p1]** to end.

Round 4 **[P1, k1]** to end.

Flared hem

With MC only, work Rounds 1–4 of Slip Stitch Pattern twice more. Bind off.

Bind off as follows: K2tog, **[slip stitch back to left needle, k2tog]** to end. Fasten off.

FINISHING

Sew first few rows at together at waist.

Cut elastic to desired length plus 1". Weave elastic through elongated stitches at knit waistband; overlap and sew ends together.

OR

See page 8 to attach repurposed top to skirt.

my in·the· Groove skirts

Traditional with a twist, this almost-classic skirt features a flattering slanted hemline with a double-the-stitches ruffle. The drawstring waist allows for a comfortable fit. This skirt is very easy to make any length.

The two skirts are almost identical twins but the taupe skirt is shorter and uses the directions for a more slanted hemline. Its ruffle shows the opposite side of the purple skirt's stitch pattern. Wash and dry either skirt and you will have the queen of drape and softness!

A 33 (36, **39**, 42, **45½**, 48½)"
approximately 6" below waist, after 8 increase rounds

B 28 (30½, **33½**, 37, **40**, 43)"

C 37½ (39, **40½**, 44, **47**, 50)" *circumference before ruffle*
  75 (78, **81½**, 87½, **94**, 100)" *ruffle circumference*

Numbers in parentheses are for the taupe skirt, the others for the purple skirt; black numbers show measurements for purple skirt, blue numbers show measurements for taupe skirt length at longest portion of slanted hemline 26" (24").

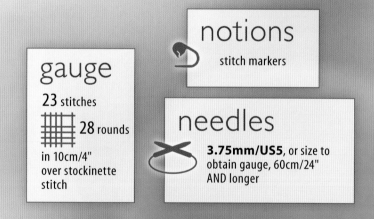

gauge

23 stitches
28 rounds
in 10cm/4"
over stockinette
stitch

notions

stitch markers

needles

3.75mm/US5, or size to obtain gauge, 60cm/24" AND longer

shaping
Increase 2 stitches at each side seam every 7 rounds, then every 4 rounds.

yarn

light weight

3

Purple skirt **800** (850, **900**, 975, **1050**, 1100) yds

Taupe skirt **775** (825, **875**, 950, **1025**, 1075) yds

Shown in Size 36: CASCADE YARNS
Ultra Pima Quatro in color 3788
Grape Groove

SKIRT

With shorter needle, cast on **160** (176, **194**, 212, **230**, 248). Beginning with a knit row, work 4 rows in stockinette stitch. After last row, turn (so reverse stockinette stitch is on RS), place marker (pm), and join to work in the round being careful not to twist stitches.

Next round: Eyelet round **[K2tog, yo]** to end.

Next round: Place side marker K**80** (88, **97**, 106, **115**, 124), pm for side, k**80** (88, **97**, 106, **115**, 124).

Rounds 1–6 Knit.

Round 7: Increase round K1, M1R, knit to 1 stitch before marker, M1L, k1, slip marker, k1, M1R, knit to 1 stitch before end of round, M1L, k1 — 4 stitches increased. Work Rounds 1–7 once more — **168** (184, **202**, 220, **238**, 256) stitches. Continue in stockinette stitch, working Increase Round every 4 rounds **12** (10, **8**, 8, **8**, 8) more times — **216** (224, **234**, 252, **270**, 288) stitches. Work even in stockinette stitch until piece measures 17" (14"), or 5½" from desired length.

Short-row section

There are 2 options for the short rows; the blue number results in a short-row section that is 1" deeper and in a slightly more slanted hemline as seen on the taupe skirt.

SR 1, 2 Knit to **9** (**8**) before end of round, wrap and turn (W&T); purl to **9** (**8**) before end of round, W&T.

SR 3, 4 Knit to **9** (**8**) before last wrap, W&T; purl to **9** (**8**) before last wrap, W&T.

Repeat SR 3 and 4 until last wrap is fewer than **9** (**8**) stitches before side marker, knit to side marker, cut yarn.

Slip stitches back to left needle until beginning of round is reached. Rejoin yarn. Knit 1 round, hiding wraps (see box). Purl 1 round. Change to longer needle. *Next round* **[K1, yo]** to end — **432** (448, **468**, 504, **540**, 576) stitches.

Ruffle

Purl 1 round. *Next round* **[K3 (p3), p1 (k1)]** to end. Repeat until this portion measures 5½", or desired length. Bind off in pattern.

FINISHING

Sew first few rows together at waist.

See page 9 for drawstring options

See page 9 for drawstring options

notes

1 For unfamiliar abbreviations and techniques, see page 116.

2 For purple skirt, use black numbers throughout. For Taupe skirt, use blue numbers if given, black numbers if not.

variations

V1 · Use a simple knit/purl combination for the main part of the skirt.

V2 · Substitute a lace pattern for the written ruffle pattern. It's easy to adjust the stitch count for the required multiple within the increase eyelet row.

To hide wraps

Candace suggests you try this: With the right needle lift the wrap up and over the stitch on the left needle so the wrap is the second stitch from the tip of the needle. Slip the stitch knitwise. Slip it back purlwise. Knit the stitch and the wrap together through the back loop.

Shown in Size 39: GREEN MOUNTAIN SPINNERY Sylvan Spirit in color Moonshadow

my mondrian skirt

Inspired by the artwork masterpieces of Dutch painter, Piet Mondrian, this skirt offers bold graphic lines and bright colors. Traditionally A-line, it is worked in two pieces and offers a knit-in elastic casing at the waist.

gauge

26 stitches

42 rows

in 10cm/4" over stockinette stitch

notions

¾" elastic to fit waist

needles

3.25mm/US3, or size to obtain gauge, 60cm/24" or longer

B

↓

A

C

25"

A 35 (**40**, 42, 44, **46**, 48)" *approximately 6" below waist*

B 30 (30, **32**, 34, **36**, 38)"

C 42 (**44**, 47, 49, **52**, 54)", *circumference after last increase round*

shaping

Skirt is worked in 2 pieces: a front and a back. Increase 1 stitch at each side of each piece.

Shown in Size 35: Sock yarn in Black (MC), Yellow (A), Blue (B), Red (C), and White (D)

KNIT my SKIRT

yarn

super fine weight
MC 500 (525, **550**, 575, **625**, 650) yds
A 100 (105, **115**, 120, **125**, 130) yds
B and C 165 (175, **185**, 195, **205**, 215)
yds each
D 190 (200, **215**, 225, **235**, 245) yds

FRONT/BACK *MAKE TWO*

Make 1 using each Color Arrangement.

Waistband

With MC, cast on **98** (98, **104**, 112, **118**, 124).

Row 1 (WS) Knit.

Row 2 (RS) **[K1, yo 3 times]** to last stitch, k1.

Row 3 Knit, dropping all yos from previous row.

Work 4 rows in stockinette stitch.

Body

Begin chart: Row 1 (RS) K2 (2, **5**, 9, **12**, 15) in MC, place marker (pm), work Row 1 of Chart following one of the Color Arrangements, pm, knit MC to end.

Row 2 (WS) Purl in colors as established.

Continue in stockinette stitch as established, working Chart in colors indicated by Color Arrangement and working beginning and ending stitches in MC AND At SAME TIME, Inc 1 each side every **6** (4, **4**, 4, **4**) rows **16** (18, **20**, 20, **22**, 22) times, then every 12 rows 4 times — **40** (44, **48**, 48, **52**, 52) stitches increased; **138** (142, **152**, 160, **170**, 176) stitches.

At end of chart, work 2 rows MC.

Hem

Row 1: Turning ridge (RS) Purl.

Row 2 Purl.

Row 3: Decrease row K**5** (3, **3**, 3, **3**, 2), k2tog, **[k12 (13, 14, 15, 16, 17), k2tog]** 9 times, knit to end — **128** (132, **142**, 150, **160**, 166) stitches.

Next 13 rows Work even in stockinette.

Bind off loosely.

Finishing

Sew side seams. Fold hem to WS along turning ridge and sew in place. Cut elastic to desired length plus 1". Weave through elongated stitches at waistband; overlap and sew ends together.

plan your own

You can work a bottom band of MC or make up a few more color blocks until desired length is reached.

Variation

Recolor the Color Arrangements. Even though Mondrian did not use green in his geometric paintings, Candace did; her original version used green rather than white.

notes

1 For unfamiliar abbreviations and techniques, see page 116.

2 Use a separate length of yarn for each block of color. Bring new color under the old at color change to prevent holes.

Inc 1

Work all increases in MC.

At beginning of RS row
K2, M1L.

At end of RS row Work to last 2 stitches, M1R, k2.

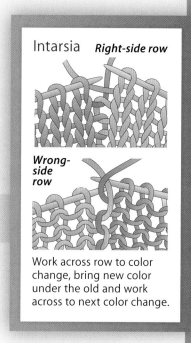

Intarsia **Right-side row**

Wrong-side row

Work across row to color change, bring new color under the old and work across to next color change.

Chart

Column 1 (30 stitches):
- 32
- 34
- 9 | 3 | 12 | 18
- 12
- 26
- 36
- 18 | 12 | 3 | 9
- 4 | 12 | 3
- 22 | 3

Column 2 (28 stitches):
- 7 | 3 | 12 | 18
- 20
- 22
- 30
- 18 | 12 | 3 | 7
- 26
- 22 | 4
- 42 | 3

Column 3 (30 stitches):
- 20
- 18 | 12 | 3 | 9
- 26
- 16
- 32
- 9 | 3 | 12 | 18
- 34
- 34 | 4

Row 2 ←   Row 1 →

3 *Vertical numbers refer to stitches.*

4 *Horizontal numbers refer to rows.*

☐ *Work in MC, 3 stitches for vertical dividers,
4 rows for horizontal dividers.*

Color arrangements

Color key
☐ MC ☐ A ▨ B ■ C ☐ D

A side-to-side skirt is always a treat—just knit until it wraps around you. It's that easy to try on: hold it up to your waist; when it goes around, it is finished!

The cast-on determines the length of the skirt: to make it shorter, just cast on fewer stitches.

Short rows create the series of wedges that fit together to make an A-line skirt, so shaping is a bit more tricky. For the waist to be narrower than the hemline, fewer rows are worked at the top of the skirt, more rows at the bottom.

Probably one of the main advantages of side-to-side construction is that vertical stripes—whether of color or texture—can be achieved easily without working several colors or stitch patterns on the same row.

These skirts are worked in rows, not rounds. If you prefer knitting back and forth to knitting circularly, and if you enjoy shaping with short rows, side-to-side skirts are for you!

side to side

my sideways glance skirt

This skirt is knit from the hem to the waist, in two pieces. A 4" stockinette-stitch yoke makes the waist totally flat. The seams of the skirt are invisible thanks to the ridge pattern that meets up perfectly at the sides. The waist has ½" elastic sewn to the top of the yoke.

shaping

Skirt is shaped with short-row wedges:
Each repeat of Ridge Pattern adds 6 stockinette-stitch rows at the top AND 14 stockinette-stitch rows plus 1 garter ridge at the bottom.

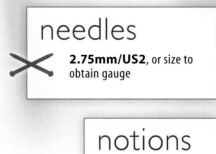

23"

A 36½ (38, **40**, 42, **44**, 45½, **47½**, 49½, **51**)"
approximately 5" below waist

B 26½ (28, **29**, 30½, **32**, 33, **34½**, 36, **37**)"

C 58 (61, **64**, 67, **70**, 73, **76**, 79, **82**)"

needles

✕ **2.75mm/US2**, or size to obtain gauge

notions

stitch marker

½" elastic to fit waist

gauge

22 stitches

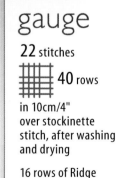

40 rows

in 10cm/4" over stockinette stitch, after washing and drying

16 rows of Ridge Pattern (including short rows) = 1½" at widest point

yarn

 fine weight
1150 (1200, **1275**, 1325, **1375**, 1450, **1500**, 1575, **1625**) yds

Shown in Size 38: FIESTA YARNS
Linnette in color Candy Apple Red

SKIRT HALF *MAKE 2*

Cast on 126 loosely. Purl 1 row; knit 1 row.
Work Rows 1–16 of Ridge Pattern a total of **19** (20, **21**, 22, **23**, 24, **25**, 26, **27**) times. Purl 1 row. Bind off on RS in knit.

FINISHING
Bottom edging

With RS facing and starting at a side seam, pick up and knit 9 stitches within each Ridge Pattern repeat — **342** (360, **378**, 396, **414**, 432, **450**, 468, **486**) stitches. Place marker (pm) and join to work in the round.

Purl 5 rounds; turn. Bind off on WS as follows: **[K2tog through back loops, slip the stitch on the right needle to the left needle purlwise]** to end. Fasten off.

Sew side seams.
See page 9 to attach elastic to skirt with herringbone-stitch.
Machine wash and dry.

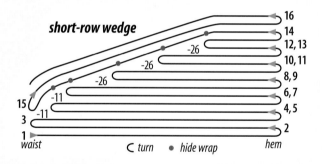

short-row wedge

waist   C *turn* • *hide wrap*   *hem*

To adjust length

Add or subtract stitches (up to 20) at the hem. Make the same adjustment to the bold numbers in the Ridge Pattern.

note

For unfamiliar abbreviations and techniques, see page 116.

Ridge Pattern

Row 1 (WS) P22, k**103**, p1.
Row 2 (RS) Knit.
Row 3 Purl.
Begin Short rows: SR 4, 5 K**115**, wrap and turn (W&T), purl to end.
SR 6, 7 K**104**, W&T, purl to end.
SR 8, 9 K**78**, W&T, purl to end.
SR 10, 11 K**52**, W&T, purl to end.
SR 12, 13 K**26**, W&T, purl to end.
Row 14 K1, p**103**, purling each wrap together with the wrapped stitch; k22, knitting each wrap together with the wrapped stitch.
Row 15 Purl.
Row 16 Knit.

To hide the wraps

Candace suggests you try this:
To purl the wrap together with the wrapped stitch:
Lift wrap up and over so it is behind the original stitch. Slip the original stitch knitwise, slip the stitch purlwise back to the left needle. Purl through the backs of the stitch and the wrap together.
To knit the wrap together with the wrapped stitch:
Lift wrap up and over stitch so it is behind the original stitch. Work an SSK with the stitch and the wrap.

my Stripes at Dusk skirt

This skirt is a cousin to My Sideways Glance Skirt. It is longer, has a more sleek fit, and uses two colors.

shaping

Skirt is shaped with short-row wedges: Each 18-row repeat adds 8 stockinette-stitch rows at the waist AND 14 stockinette-stitch rows plus 2 garter ridges at the hem.

sizing

Because this skirt is worked sideways, it is super easy to make bigger or smaller. Work the 18-row repeat for each section until the skirt is the desired size. Each repeat adds approximately 1½" at the hip.

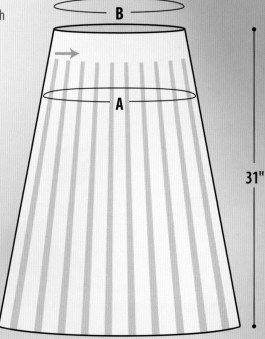

yarn

fine weight
MC 1000 (1075, **1150**, 1225, **1310**, 1375, **1450**) yds
CC 270 (290, **310**, 335, **360**, 375, **395**) yds

Shown in Size 35: LOUET Euroflax Sport Weight Linen in colors Charcoal (MC) and Black (CC)

A 35 (38, **40**, 43, **46**, 48, **51**)"
approximately 6" below waist

B 24 (25, **27**, 29, **31**, 32, **34**)"

C 52 (56, **60**, 64, **68**, 72, **76**)"

gauge

20 stitches

36 rows

in 10cm/4"
over stockinette
stitch, after
washing and
drying

needles

2.75mm/US2, or size to
obtain gauge, 60cm/24"

notions

¾" elastic to fit waist

my Flock of sheep skirt

gauge

22 stitches

52 rows

in 10cm/4"
over garter stitch,
using larger needle

notions

3/8" elastic to
fit waist

needles

3.25mm/US3, or size to
obtain gauge, 60cm/24"
AND
2.75mm/US2, 60cm/24"

shaping

Short-row panels at sides shape body of skirt.
Short-row godets add flare at hem.

Shown in Size 36: BROWN SHEEP Nature
Spun Fingering in colors 225F Brick Road
(MC), 601F Pepper (A), 880F Charcoal (B),
N03F Grey Heather (C), 701F Stone (D), 123F
Saddle Tan (E), 720F Ash (F), N91F Aran (G)

This skirt came about as an intarsia antidote to the Mondrian skirt...fewer colors per row are used, as this skirt is worked lengthwise. It proved to be a most satisfying knit and fit.

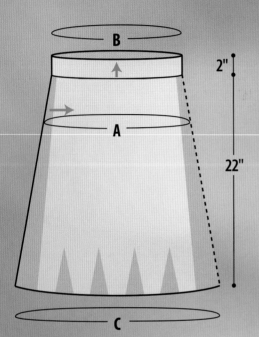

A 36 (39, **42**, 45, **48½**, 51½, **54½**)"
approximately 6" below waist

B 26 (28½, **31**, 33½, **36**, 38½, **41**)"

C 73½ (76½, **79½**, 83, **86**, 89, **92**)"

yarn

super fine weight

MC 500 (525, **550**, 600, **650**, 675, **700**) yds
A, C, F and G 75 (75, **75**, 75, **80**, 85, **90**) yds each
B and D 125 (125, **125**, 135, **140**, 150, **155**) yds each
E 225 (225, **230**, 240, **255**, 270, **280**) yds

notes

1 For unfamiliar abbreviations and techniques, see page 116.

2 Skirt is worked sideways, entirely in garter stitch; all RS rows begin at hemline.

3 All rows begin with a slip stitch.

4 To change colors, the last stitch of the last row is knit with the new color as follows: Take the tail of the old color and bring it forward, take the tail of the new color and leave it forward, bring the new color to the back and knit the last stitch.

5 Use a separate length of yarn for each block of color. Bring new color under the old at color change to prevent holes (see page 70).

PIECE A
Beginning panel

With larger needle, waste yarn, and using a temporary cast-on, cast on 121. With MC, knit 1 row. ***Next row*** (WS) Sl 1, k10, k2tog, knit to end—120 stitches.

Begin short rows: SR 1, 2 Sl 1, knit to last 4 stitches, turn; yo, knit to end.

SR 3, 4 Sl 1, knit to 4 stitches before last yo, turn; yo right needle, knit to end.

Repeat SR 3, 4 ten more times—12 yos and 72 stitches before the last yo.

Next 16 SR Sl 1, knit to 8 before last yo, turn; yo, knit to end.

Next row Sl 1, knit to end, hiding yos.

Last WS row of beginning panel Sl 1, knit to last stitch, cut MC, bring tail of MC forward, leave tail of A forward, bring A to the back and knit the last stitch.

Panel I

50 C	63 B	7A

Row 1 (RS) With A, sl 1, k6; with B, k63; with C, k50.

Row 2 (WS) With C, sl 1, k49; with B, k63; with A, k7—1 ridge completed.

Repeat Rows 1 and 2 for a total of **19** (21, **23**, 25, **27**, 29, **31**) ridges. Cut all yarns.

MC Godet

Rows 1 and 2 With MC, sl 1, knit to end.

Begin short rows: SR 3, 4 Sl 1, k2, turn; yo, knit to end.

SR 5, 6 Sl 1, k2, hide yo, k2, turn; yo, knit to end.

SR 7, 8 Sl 1, knit to next yo, hide yo, k2, turn; yo, knit to end.

Repeat SR 7, 8 until there are 36 stitches on right needle, turn; yo, knit to end.

In a nutshell, for each pair of short rows: Sl 1, knit to yo, work the yo and stitch after it together, knit 2 more stitches, turn; yo, knit to end.

The next set of short rows is a mirror image of those for the first half of the godet.

SR 1, 2 Sl 1, k32, turn; yo, knit to end.

SR 3, 4 Sl 1, k29, turn; yo, knit to end.

SR 5, 6 Sl 1, knit to 3 before last yo, turn; yo, knit to end.

Repeat SR 5, 6 until you end with sl 1, k2, turn; yo, knit to end.

Next row Sl 1, knit to end, hiding yos.

Last WS row of godet Sl 1, knit to end.

Panel 2

80 E	27 G	13A

With A, sl 1, k12; with G, k27; with E; k80. Work as for Panel 1. Work MC Godet.

Panel 3

30 F	71 D	19A

With A, sl 1, k18; with D, k71; with F, k30. Work as for Panel 1. Work MC Godet.

Panel 4

80 E	27 G	13A

Work as for Panel 2. Work MC Godet.

Panel 5

50 C	63 B	7A

Work as for Panel 1.

Ending panel

Row 1 With MC, sl 1, knit to end. ***Row 2*** Sl 1, knit to end.

Begin short rows: SR 1, 2 Sl 1, k7, turn; yo, knit to end.

Next 16 SR Sl 1, knit to yo, hide yo, k7, turn; yo, knit to end—72 stitches on right needle after the last yo; 48 stitches remain for the rest of the short rows.

Next 22 SR Sl 1, knit to yo, hide yo, k3, turn; yo, knit to end.

Next row Sl 1, knit to end, hiding yo, k3.

Last WS row of ending panel Sl 1, knit to end. Cut yarn, leaving a 3-yd tail to be used for 3-needle bind-off.

variations

V1 · Instead of blocks of colors, add more colors lengthwise by knitting a few ridges of each panel in a different color.

V2 · To make the skirt longer, add stitches to the original cast-on in increments of 8. This will give more short rows to the side panels; you will have to decide where to distribute those extra stitches within the blocks of colors.

PIECE B

Work Beginning Panel.

Panel 1

83 D	30 F	7A

With A, sl 1, k6; with F, k30; with D, k83. Work as for Piece A, Panel 1. Work MC Godet.

Panel 2

37 G	70 E	13 A

With A, sl 1, k12; with E, k70; with G, k37. Work as for Panel 1. Work MC Godet.

Panel 3

30 C	71 B	19 A

With A, sl 1, k18; with B, k71; with C, k30. Work as for Panel 1. Work MC Godet.

Panel 4

37 G	70 E	13 A

Work as for Panel 2. Work MC Godet.

Panel 5

83 D	30 F	7A

Work as for Panel 1.
Work Ending Panel.

SIDE SEAMS

Carefully remove waste yarn, placing live stitches onto smaller needle. With WS together and attached 3-yd MC tail, join Piece A and Piece B using 3-needle bind-off.

KNIT YOKE

With smaller needle, MC, RS facing, and starting at one of the side seams, pick up and knit (PUK) 1 stitch in each of the slipped edge stitches—**214** (234, **254**, 274, **294**, 314, **334**) stitches. Place marker and join to work in the round.

Knit 1 round.

Work in k1, p1 rib for 5 rounds.

First decrease round **[K1, p1]** twice, **[k2tog, p2tog, (k1, p1) 3 times]** to end—**172** (188, **204**, 220, **236**, 250, **268**) stitches.

Work in established rib for 5 rounds.

Second decrease round K1, p1, **[K2tog, p2tog, (k1, p1) 5 times]** to last **0** (4, **6**, 8, **10**, 10, **0**) stitches, work to end in established rib—**148** (162, **176**, 190, **204**, 216, **230**) stitches.

Work in established rib for 2 rounds.

Next round: Eyelet round **[K2tog, yo]** to last stitch, k1.

Next 3 rounds **[K1, p1]** to end.

Bind off very loosely.

FINISHING

Cut elastic to desired length plus 1". Weave through eyelets in yoke; overlap and sew ends together.

Hiding yos

On a RS row, SSK (yo together with next stitch).

Sl 1

With yarn in front, slip stitch purlwise, then take yarn between needles to back of work (do not wrap yarn around side of first stitch).

sheep

my Ruffles have ridges skirt

gauge

21 stitches

 48 rows

in 10cm/4"
over garter stitch,
using larger needle

yarn

 fine weight

1325 (1400, **1500**, 1575, **1675**, 1750, **1850**) yds

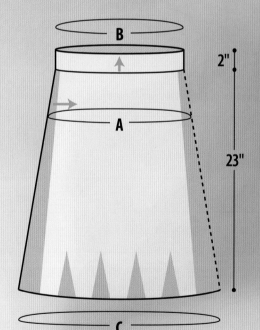

A 39 (42½, **45½**, 49, **52½**, 55½, **59**)"
approximately 6" below waist

B 28 (30½, **33½**, 36, **38½**, 41½, **44**)"

C 79½ (83, **86½**, 89½, **93**, 96½, **99½**)"

By working the exact same directions
as for *My Flock of Sheep Skirt*, but
using color-gradient yarn and no knitter-
controlled color changes, you get a skirt
with vertical columns of color—the yarn
does it all for you!

Shown in Size 39: KAUNI
Effektgarn in color ET

bottom up

Bottom up requires a bit more advance planning than top down. You need to decide about the bottom circumference of the skirt before you cast on, and you have to know exactly what your hemline is going to look like, as there's no opportunity to play around with it once you are halfway up the skirt. You will have to decide how you will do the decreasing, if any, between hemline and hip. You will also need to know the approximate finished length of the skirt, as you will need to begin the waist decreases at the hip—usually about 7 inches below the top of the skirt.

It's a little trickier to try on a bottom-up skirt while it's in process, but it can be done. Enlist someone to help you hold the skirt up while you try it on.

If you are unsure about yarn amounts, this blueprint could prove stressful.

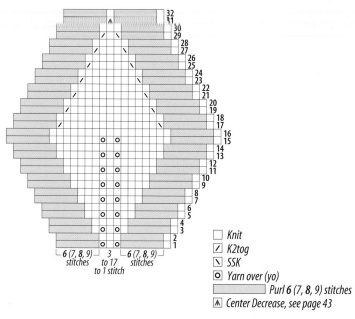

□ Knit
☑ K2tog
◩ SSK
⊙ Yarn over (yo)
▨ Purl 6 (7, 8, 9) stitches
▲ Center Decrease, see page 43

├ 6 (7, 8, 9) ┤ 3 ├ 6 (7, 8, 9) ┤
stitches   to 17   stitches
            to 1 stitch

Leaf 1

Round 1 Yo, k1, yo.
All even-numbered rounds Knit.
Round 3 K1, yo, k1, yo, k1. **Round 5** K2, yo, k1, yo, k2.
Round 7 K3, yo, k1, yo, k3. **Round 9** K4, yo, k1, yo, k4.
Round 11 K5, yo, k1, yo, k5. **Round 13** K6, yo, k1, yo, k6.
Round 15 K7, yo, k1, yo, k7. **Round 17** SSK, k13, k2tog.
Round 19 SSK, k11, k2tog. **Round 21** SSK, k9, k2tog.
Round 23 SSK, k7, k2tog. **Round 25** SSK, k5, k2tog.
Round 27 SSK, k3, k2tog. **Round 29** SSK, k1, k2tog.
Round 31 Center Decrease.

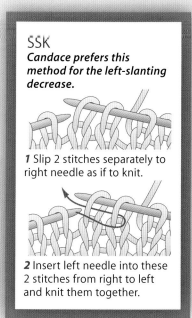

SSK

Candace prefers this method for the left-slanting decrease.

1 Slip 2 stitches separately to right needle as if to knit.

2 Insert left needle into these 2 stitches from right to left and knit them together.

note

For unfamiliar abbreviations and techniques, see page 116.

SKIRT

With larger needle, cast on **126** (144, **162**, 180) for front, place marker (pm) for side, cast on **126** (144, **162**, 180) for back, pm for beginning of round—**252** (288, **324**, 360) stitches. Join to work in the round, being careful not to twist stitches.

Section 1

Begin Leaf 1: Round 1 *[K1, p6 (7, 8, 9)] four times, [k1, p6 (7, 8, 9), work Leaf 1, p6 (7, 8, 9)] five times, [k1, p6 (7, 8, 9)] four times; repeat from * once more. Continue as established through Round 32 of Leaf 1.

Section 2

Begin Leaf 2: Round 1 *[K1, p6 (7, 8, 9)] five times, [k1, p6 (7, 8, 9), work Leaf 2, p6 (7, 8, 9)] four times, [k1, p6 (7, 8, 9)] five times; repeat from * once more. Continue as established through remainder of Leaf 2.

Chart note

For Leaf 2, the center 4 rounds of Leaf 1 are not worked. Each subsequent section of leaves eliminates 4 more rounds.

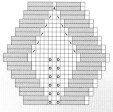

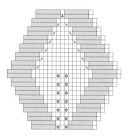

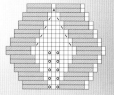

Leaf 2

Work Leaf 1 Rounds 1–14, then Rounds 19–32.

Leaf 3

Work Leaf 1 Rounds 1–12, then Rounds 21–32.

Leaf 4

Work Leaf 1 Rounds 1–10, then Rounds 23–32.

Leaf 5

Work Leaf 1 Rounds 1–8, then Rounds 25–32.

DEC 2
K1, SSP, p2 (3, **4**, 5), p2tog.

Section 3
Begin Leaf 3: Round 1 *[**K1, p6 (7, 8, 9)**] six times, [**k1, p6 (7, 8, 9), work Leaf 3, p6 (7, 8, 9)**] three times, [**k1, p6 (7, 8, 9)**] six times; repeat from * once more. Continue as established through remainder of Leaf 3.

Section 4
Begin Leaf 4: Round 1 *[**K1, p6 (7, 8, 9)**] seven times, [**k1, p6 (7, 8, 9), work Leaf 3, p6 (7, 8, 9)**] twice, [**k1, p6 (7, 8, 9)**] seven times; repeat from * once more. Continue as established through remainder of Leaf 4.

Section 5
Begin Leaf 5: Round 1 *[**K1, p6 (7, 8, 9)**] eight times, [**k1, p6 (7, 8, 9), work Leaf 2, p6 (7, 8, 9)**], [**k1, p6 (7, 8, 9)**] eight times; repeat from * once more. Continue as established through remainder of Leaf 5.

Work even in established rib until piece measures 13".
> *Length can be added here.*

Begin decreasing
> *Skirt consists of 36 sections of k1, p6 (7, 8, 9) rib; 18 sections between each set of markers.*

Decrease round 1 [**Dec 2 in next section, work to 7 (8, 9, 10) stitches before marker, Dec 2 in next section, slip marker (sm)**] twice — **244** (280, **316**, 352) stitches. Mark each of the four decrease sections.
Work 4 rounds even in established rib.

Decrease round 2 [**Work marked section, Dec 2 in next section, work to 1 section before next marked section, Dec 2 in next section, work to marker, sm**] twice — **236** (272, **308**, 344) stitches. Move markers to new decrease sections.
Work 4 rounds even in established rib.

Decrease round 3 [**Work up to and including marked section, Dec 2 in next section, work to 1 section before next marked section, Dec 2 in next section, work to marker, sm**] twice — 8 stitches decreased. Move markers to new decrease sections.

Repeat Decrease Round 3 every 5 rounds 6 more times — **180** (216, **252**, 288) stitches. Remove decrease markers.
Work 7 rounds even in established rib.

Decrease round 4 [**K1, p1 (2, 2, 3), p2tog, p1 (1, 2, 2)**] to end — **144** (180, **216**, 252) stitches.
Work 3 rounds even in established rib.
Change to smaller needle.
SIZES 36, 48 ONLY Next round [**K1, p1**] to end.
SIZE 42 ONLY Next round [**K1, p3, k1**] to end.
SIZE 54 ONLY Next round [**(K1, p1) 3 times, k1**] to end.
ALL SIZES Work 3 rounds even in established rib.
Next round: Eyelet round [**K2tog, yo**] to end.
Work 3 more rounds in established rib for each size.
Bind off loosely.

FINISHING
See page 9 for drawstring options.
> *Because the yarn has some elastic in it, this works out well.*

93

MY Autumn leaves SKIRT

gauge

27 stitches

||||| 34 rounds

in 10cm/4"
over k1, p6 rib, using
larger needles

needles

3.5mm/US4, or size to
obtain gauge, 60cm/24"
or longer
AND
circular needle 1 or 2
sizes smaller

notions

stitch markers

5.5mm/I-9

A 33 (38, **42½**, 47½)"
*approximately 5" below waist, before first
decrease round*

B 23½ (28½, **33**, 38)" *unstretched*

shaping
Decreases are worked in purl rib
every 4 rounds as shown.

21"

For My Silver Leaf Skirt, leaves
are gathered into 2 triangles of
graduated size. Here, 3 tiers of
leaves circle the hem.

yarn

fine weight
2 **1400** (1650, **1875**, 2125) yds

Shown in Size 33: HIKOO
CoBaSi in color 053 Cabernet

95

SKIRT

With larger needle, cast on **112** (128, **144**, 160) for front, place marker (pm) for side, cast on **112** (128, **144**, 160) for back, pm for beginning of round — **224** (256, **288**, 320) stitches. Join to work in the round, being careful not to twist stitches.

Section 1

Begin Leaf 3: Round 1 *[**K1, p6 (7, 8, 9)**] twice, work Leaf 3, p**6** (7, **8**, 9), k1, p**6** (7, **8**, 9); repeat from *7 more times. Continue as established through remainder of Leaf 3. Work 5 rounds even in established rib.

Section 2

Begin Leaf 4: Round 1 * Work Leaf 4, p**6** (7, **8**, 9), [**k1, p6 (7, 8, 9)**] three times; repeat from * 7 more times. Continue as established through remainder of Leaf 4. Work 5 rounds even in established rib.

Section 3

Work as for Section 1 EXCEPT work Leaf 5. Work even in established rib until piece measures 16", or 5" from desired length.

Begin decreasing

Skirt consists of 32 sections of k1, p6 (7, 8, 9) rib; 16 sections between each set of markers.

Decrease round 1 **[Dec 2 in next section, work to 7 (8, 9, 10) stitches before marker, Dec 2 in next section, slip marker (sm)]** twice—**244** (280, **316**, 352) stitches. Mark each of the 4 decrease sections. Work 3 rounds even in established rib.

Decrease round 2 **[Work marked section, Dec 2 in next section, work to 1 section before next marked section, Dec 2 in next section, work to marker, sm]** twice — **208** (240, **272**, 304) stitches. Move markers to new decrease sections. Work 3 rounds even in established rib.

Decrease round 3 **[Work up to and including marked section, Dec 2 in next section, work to 1 section before next marked section, Dec 2 in next section, work to marker, sm]** twice—8 stitches decreased. Move markers to new decrease sections.

note

For unfamiliar abbreviations and techniques, see page 116.

LEAF PATTERNS

See charts below and written instructions on page 92.

DEC 2

K1, SSP, p**2** (3, **4**, 5), p2tog.

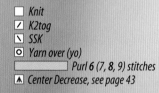

☐ Knit
◪ K2tog
◩ SSK
⊙ Yarn over (yo)
▭ Purl 6 (7, 8, 9) stitches
▲ Center Decrease, see page 43

Leaf 3

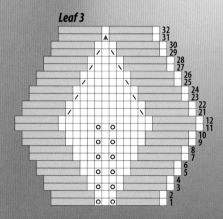

Repeat Decrease Round 3 every 4 rounds 5 more times — **160** (192, **224**, 256) stitches. Remove decrease markers.

Work 3 rounds even in established rib.

Next decrease round **[K1, p1 (2, 2, 3), p2tog, p1 (1, 2, 2)]** to end — **128** (160, **192**, 224) stitches.

Work 3 rounds even in established rib.

Change to smaller needle.

SIZES 33, 42½ ONLY **Next round** **[K1, p1]** to end.

SIZE 38 ONLY **Next round** **[K1, p3, k1]** to end.

SIZE 47½ ONLY **Next round** **[(K1, p1) 3 times, k1]** to end.

ALL SIZES Work 3 rounds even in established rib.

Next round: Eyelet round **[K2tog, yo]** to end.

Work 3 rounds even in established rib for each size.

Bind off loosely.

FINISHING

See page 9 for drawstring options.

Because the yarn has some elastic in it, this works out well.

Leaf 4

Leaf 5

Seashells skirt

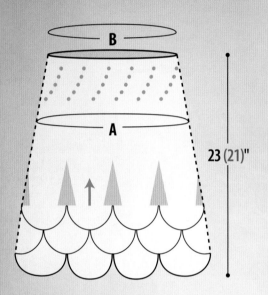

23 (21)"

Oh, glorious purple; oh, beautiful scallops! Three tiers of scallop shells grace the hemline of this skirt, continuing their ribbed pattern to the waist. Because this skirt is basically ribbing, it can fit a wide variety of sizes by being stretched a little or a lot, depending on how you wish the fit to be. Here is an irresistible opportunity to buy a pair of purple undies to use for the waistband!

A 40 (45, **50**)" slightly stretched; collapses to **30** (36, **42**)" *approximately 5" below waist*

B 24 (28½, **33**)"

C 48 (54, **60**)"

· shaping

Decreases are worked within the purl ribs every 6 rounds.

needles

3.75mm/US5, or size to obtain gauge, 60cm/24" or longer
AND
2mm/US0

gauge

24 stitches

28 rounds

in 10cm/4" over k2, p2 rib, slightly stretched

each scallop = 4½" x 6"

yarn

super fine weight
MC 875 (1000, **1125**) yds
A 225 (250, **300**) yds
B 175 (**200**, **225**) yds

notions

stitch marker

¾" elastic to fit waist
OR
2½" repurposed top

Shown in Size 36: CASCADE YARNS Heritage in colors 5650 Lavender (MC), 5633 Italian Plum (A), and 5625 Purple Hyacinth (B)

Scallop border

I Make **8** (9, **10**) A Scallops.

2 With B, pick up and knit (PUK) into slipped stitches of 2 A Scallops: starting at top of one A Scallop (not including held stitch), PUK23 down left edge, loop cast on 1, PUK23 up right edge of second A Scallop — 47 stitches. Complete B Scallop to join the pair.

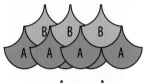

Continue to make B Scallops, joining **3** (3, **4**) pairs of A Scallops.

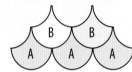

For size 45, one A Scallop remains, join it onto a pair for a triplet.

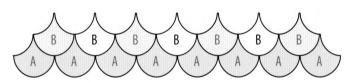

3 Continue working B Scallops, joining pairs (and triplet), forming a band.

4 Work 1 more B Scallop, joining into a ring.

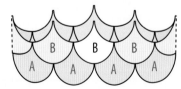

notes

1 For unfamiliar abbreviations and techniques, see page 116.

2 For KNIT WAISTBAND, use black numbers throughout.

3 For REPURPOSED TOP, use blue numbers if given, black numbers if not.

Sl 1

With yarn in front, slip stitch purlwise, then take yarn between needles to back of work (do not wrap yarn around side of first stitch).

Scallop

Work all scallops with larger needles. For A Scallops, cast on 47 with A; for B Scallops, PUK and cast on with B.

Row 1 (WS) Sl 1, knit to end.

Row 2 (RS) Sl 1, k1, SSK, yo, k39, yo, k2tog, k2.

Row 3 Sl 1, **[k10, k2tog]** 3 times, knit to end — 44 stitches.

Row 4 Sl 1, k2, **[yo, k2tog]** to last 3 stitches, yo, k3 — 45 stitches.

Row 5: Begin rib Sl 1, k4, **[p2, k2]** to last 4, k2tog, k2 — 44 stitches.

Row 6 Sl 1, k1, SSK, yo, SSK, work in established rib to last 6, k2tog, yo, k2tog, k2 — 2 stitches decreased.

Row 7 Sl 1, k2, p2, work in established rib to last 5, p2, k3.

Rows 8–37 Repeat Rows 6 and 7 fifteen times — 12 stitches.

Row 38 Sl 1, k2, SSK, k2, k2tog, k3 — 10 stitches.

Row 39 Sl 1, k2, p4, k3.

Row 40 Sl 1, k2, SSK, k2tog, k3 — 8 stitches.

Rows 41, 43, and 45 Sl 1, knit to end.

Row 42 Sl 1, k1, SSK, k2tog, k2 — 6 stitches.

Row 44 Sl 1, SSK, k2tog, k1 — 4 stitches.

Row 46 Slip 2 together knitwise, k2tog, pass the slipped stitches over the k2tog. Place remaining stitch on hold. Cut yarn, leaving a 5" tail.

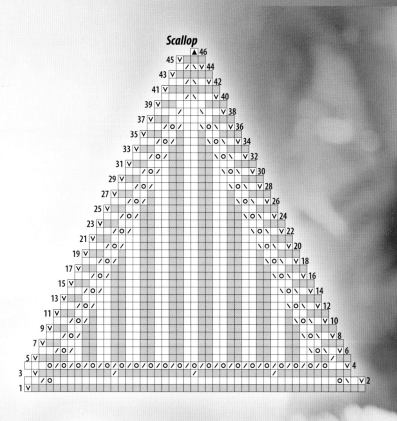

Scallop

Stitch key

- ☐ Knit on RS, purl on WS
- ▨ Purl on RS, knit on WS
- ◉ Yarn over (yo)
- ◩ SSK
- ◪ K2tog
- Ⅴ Sl 1 purlwise with yarn at RS of work
- ▲ Sl 2 together knitwise, k2tog, p2sso

*After working decrease on Row 46,
place remaining stitch on hold.
Cut yarn, leaving a 5" tail.*

Seashells

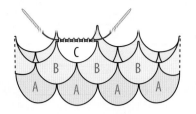 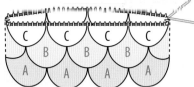

5 Work Short-row Scallops, leaving remaining stitches from each Short-row Scallop on needle.

Working yo together with next stitch

Whether to k2tog or p2tog is determined by the stitch after the yo.

On RS rows If knit, work k2tog; if purl, work p2tog.

On WS rows If knit, work SSK; if purl, work SSP.

SSP

A left-slanting single decrease

1 Slip 2 stitches separately to right needle as if to knit.

2 Slip these 2 stitches back onto left needle. Insert right needle through their 'back loops' (into the second stitch and then the first).

3 Purl them together: 2 stitches become 1.

The result is a left-slanting decrease.

Short-row Scallop

With larger needle and MC, PUK23 down left edge of one B Scallop, knit held A stitch, PUK23 up right edge of next B Scallop.

Row 1 Sl 1, **[k10, k2tog]** 3 times, knit to end—44 stitches.

Row 2 Sl 1, k2, **[yo, k2tog]** to last 3 stitches, yo, k3—45 stitches.

Row 3: Begin rib Sl 1, k4, **[p2, k2]** to last 4, k2tog, k2—44 stitches.

Begin short rows: SR 1 (RS) Sl 1, **[k2, p2]** 8 times, turn.

SR 2 (WS) Yo, **[k2, p2]** 5 times, k2, turn.

SR 3 (RS) Yo, work in pattern to yo in previous row, work yo together with next stitch, turn.

SR 4 (WS) Yo, work in pattern to yo in previous row, work yo together with next stitch, turn.

Repeat SR 3 and 4 six more times; there are 4 stitches unworked on each edge of the row just completed.

Next SR (RS) Yo, work to yo in previous row, work yo together with next stitch, k3.

Last WS row Sl 1, k2, work to last yo, work yo together with next stitch, k3, PUP2 (1 in each slipped edge stitch), W&T.

Complete scallop (RS) Work 46 stitches onto right needle, PUK2 (1 in each slipped edge stitch), knit held stitch from A Scallop.

Repeat Short-row Scallop between each pair of B Scallops—**392** (441, **490**) stitches.

The remainder of the skirt is worked with MC.

Place marker (pm), knit 1 round; purl 1 round.

Next round: Eyelet round [K2tog, yo] to last **2** (3, **2**) stitches, **k2tog** (k3tog, **k2tog**), yo—**392** (440, **490**) stitches.

Purl 1 round, M1 **zero** (one, **zero**) time—**392** (441, **490**) stitches.

Knit 1 round. At end of round, remove marker, p7, pm for new beginning of round.

This marker will remain as the last marker for the last repeat.

Next round [(K2, p2) 8 times, k2, p15, pm] **to end.**

Next 4 rounds [(K2, p2) 8 times, k2, **purl to marker**] **to end.**

Decrease round 1 [(K2, p2) 8 times, k2, p2tog, p11, SSP] **to end** — **16** (18, **20**) stitches decreased on this and every Decrease round. Work 5 rounds even.

Decrease round 2 [(K2, p2) 8 times, k2, p2tog, p9, SSP] **to end.** Work 5 rounds even.

Decrease round 3 [(K2, p2) 8 times, k2, p2tog, p7, SSP] **to end.** Work 5 rounds even.

Decrease round 4 [(K2, p2) 8 times, k2, p2tog, p5, SSP] **to end.** Work 5 rounds even.

Decrease round 5 [(K2, p2) 8 times, k2, p2tog, p3,SSP] **to end.** Work 5 rounds even.

Decrease round 6 [(K2, p2) 8 times, k2, p2tog, p1, SSP] **to end.** Work 5 rounds even.

Decrease round 7 [(K2, p2) 8 times, k2, p2tog, p1] **to end.** Work 30 rounds in k2, p2 ribbing.

Decrease round 8 [(K2, p2) 8 times, k2, SSP] **to end.** Work 10 (7) rounds even.

Decrease round 9 [K2, p2tog, (k2, p2) 7 times, k2, p1] **to end.** Work 9 (7) rounds even.

Dec round 10 [K2, p1, k2, p2tog, (k2, p2) 5 times, k2, p2tog, k2, p1] **to end.** Work 8 (5) rounds even.

Decrease round 11 [(K2, p2) twice, k2, p2tog, (k2, p2) 3 times, k2, p2tog, (k2, p1) twice] **to end.** Work 7 (5) rounds even.

Decrease round 12 [(K2, p1) 3 times, k2, p2tog, k2, p2, k2, p2tog, (k2, p1) 3 times] **to end.** Work 7 (5) rounds even.

Decrease round 13 [(K2, p1) 4 times, k2, p2tog, (k2, p1) 4 times] **to end.** Work 4 (2) rounds in k2, p1 ribbing.

Decrease round 14 [**K2tog, p1**] **to end,** removing all markers except beginning-of-round marker — 18 stitches remain in each section.

Next round [**K1, p1**] **to end.**

Change to smaller needle and work 5 rounds even.

Change to larger needle and work 1 round even.

Bind off as follows: K2, **[insert left needle through fronts of next 2 stitches on right needle and knit them together, k1]** to last stitch. Fasten off.

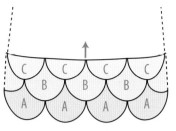

→ *direction of work*

6 Join and begin working body in rounds.

FINISHING

See page 9 to attach elastic to skirt with herringbone stitch.

OR

See page 8 to attach repurposed top to skirt.

My Mathematical Mystery Skirts

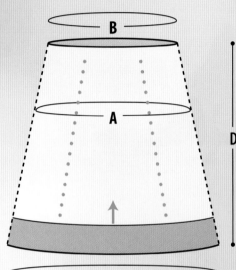

B

A

D

[ ] *Möbius hem*

A 33 (36½, **38**, 40, **42**, 45½)"
*approximately 6½" below waist, before
last 3 decrease rounds*

B 27½ (31, **32½**, 34½, **36½**, 40)"

C 54½ (58, **62**, 65½, **69**, 72½)"

D 21½ (21½, **22½**, 23½, **24**, 24)"

B

A

25"

C

[ ] *Möbius waist*

A 37 (39, **41**, 42½, **44½**, 46½)"
after Section 1, about 3" below Möbius

B 29 (31, **32½**, 34½, **36½**, 38)"
after Möbius increases

C 57½ (59, **61**, 62½, **64½**, 66½)"

*Use the intrigue of a Möbius
at the hem of your skirt!
Then, for a switch, let's put
the Möbius at the waist.
Basically the same, this skirt
is a bit fuller and longer than
its hem-up cousin.*

needles
3.75mm/US5, or size to
obtain gauge, 60cm/24"
AND 119cm/47"

AND
needle 2 sizes smaller
119cm/47"

gauge
22 stitches
34 rounds
in 10cm/4"
over stockinette
stitch, using
larger needle

notions
stitch markers

shaping
5 panels 2 stitches
decreased/increased
each panel every
8 rounds.

yarn

3
Light weight
MC 650 (700, **775**, 850, **900**, 975) yds
CC 200 (215, **230**, 240, **255**, 265) yds
MC 700 (750, **775**, 800, **825**, 875) yds
CC 125 (135, **140**, 150, **160**, 170) yds

Shown in Size 33 (37): LION BRAND
YARN LB Collection Superwash
Merino in colors 114 Cayenne (MC)
and 174 Spring Leaf (CC)

Hem-up Specifics

1 Cast on **300** (320, **340**, 360, **380**, 400).

2–4 **601** (641, **681**, 721, **761**, 801) stitches are on the double-coiled needle.

5 Knit 1 round. **[Purl 3 rounds; knit 3 rounds]** twice, ending at tail marker.

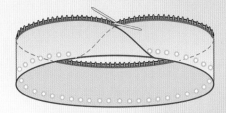

6 Bind off **300** (320, **340**, 360, **380**, 400), remove halfway marker, change to shorter needle and knit remaining 300 (320, **340**, 360, **380**, 400) stitches. Join to work in the round. Cut CC.

Twist/fold will be arranged so needle tips align to work in the round for the skirt body.

With MC, begin skirt body, following instructions on page 108.

note
For unfamiliar abbreviations and techniques, see page 116.

Candace prefers to use the loop cast-on method for a Möbius. Knitter's Magazine Spring 2015 featured Candace and editor Rick Mondragon describing options for the Möbius cast-on and discussing pros and cons. For a free download, go to www.KnittingUniverse.com/mobius

MÖBIUS CAST-ON FOR BOTH SKIRTS

The Process

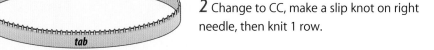

1 **Make tab** With smaller needle and waste yarn, cast on the number of stitches specified. Knit 3 rows. Cut yarn and turn.

2 Change to CC, make a slip knot on right needle, then knit 1 row.

▪▪▪ *PUK stitches*
○ *marker*

3 Slide the knitting onto the cable portion of the needle, arrange the needle and tab into a circle, and flip tab upward. Place halfway marker, then PUK into CC purl bumps of ridge …

4 … all the way to the tail. There are now 2 times the number of stitches cast on + the slip knot. Place tail marker. K2tog (slip knot with first stitch of next round), knit to tail marker.

—— *twist/fold*
······· *path from PUK*

5 Change to larger, longer needle. Work Möbius as instructed.

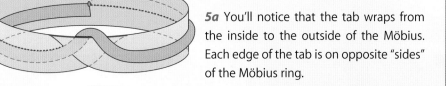

5a You'll notice that the tab wraps from the inside to the outside of the Möbius. Each edge of the tab is on opposite "sides" of the Möbius ring.

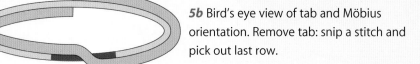

5b Bird's eye view of tab and Möbius orientation. Remove tab: snip a stitch and pick out last row.

A round is a complete trip around the double coil of the needle. Halfway through the round the tail marker will be dangling from the cable portion just below the needle points. The round is only complete when the tail marker is on the left needle tip.

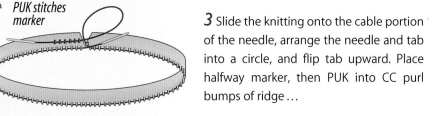
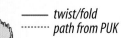

Waist-down specifics

1 Cast on **130** (140, **150**, 160, **170**, 180).

2–4 **261** (281, **301**, 321, **341**, 361) stitches are on the double-coiled needle.

5 Knit 1 round; purl 3 rounds; knit 2 rounds, ending at tail marker.

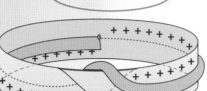

+ increase

6 *Increase round 1* **[K13 (14, 15, 16, 17, 18), M1]** to halfway marker, knit to tail marker — 10 stitches increased; **140** (150, **160**, 170, **180**, 190) stitches in first half. Purl 3 rounds.
Increase round 2 K**7** (7, **8**, 8, **9**, 9), M1, **[k14 (15, 16, 17, 18, 19), M1]** 9 times, knit to halfway marker, knit to tail marker — 10 stitches increased; **150** (160, **170**, 180, **190**, 200) stitches in first half.
Knit 1 round.

7 *Increase round 3* **[K15 (16, 17, 18, 19, 20), M1]** to halfway marker, knit to tail marker — 10 stitches increased in first half.
Next round: Make eyelets Purl to halfway marker, **[p2tog, yo]** to tail marker. Purl 1 round.

8 *Next row* Purl to halfway marker, bind off **130** (140, **150**, 160, **170**, 180) in purl, removing markers.
Change to shorter needle and, with CC, knit remaining **160** (170, **180**, 190, **200**, 210) stitches. Place marker and join to work in the round. Cut CC.

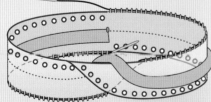

o eyelet
— bind-off

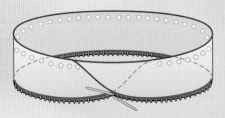

Twist/fold will be arranged so needle tips align to work in the round for the skirt body.
With MC, knit 1 round. Begin skirt body, following instructions on page 109.

Stripe Sequence

Cut CC after each CC stripe.

Work 6 rounds MC, 2 rounds CC, 12 rounds MC, 1 round CC, 1 round MC, 1 round CC, 10 rounds MC, and 1 round CC.

Work remainder of skirt in MC.

HEM-UP SKIRT BODY

While working in Stripe Sequence, continue as follows:

Set-up round [P3, k57 (61, 65, 69, 73, 77), pm] 5 times.

Use a marker of a different color for beginning-of-round marker.

Rounds 1, 3, and 5 [P3, knit to marker] to end.

Rounds 2, 4, and 6 Knit.

Round 7: Decrease round [P3, k2tog, knit to 2 before marker, SSK] to end —2 stitches decreased in each stockinette-stitch section.

Round 8 Knit.

Repeat Rounds 1–8 a total of **15** (15, **16**, 17, **18**, 18) times —**150** (170, **180**, 190, **200**, 220) stitches.

To check the fit, spread the stitches on both circular needles and try the skirt on. Stop decreasing once it is the measurement you want.

Work even for 29 rounds, or until skirt is desired length.

Purl 1 round; knit 1 round.

Next round [K2tog, yo] to end.

Knit 1 round; purl 1 round.

Bind off loosely.

FINISHING FOR BOTH SKIRTS

See page 9 for drawstring options.

WAIST-DOWN SKIRT BODY

Section 1 *NEXT 25 ROUNDS*

Set-up round **[P3, pm, k29 (31, 33, 35, 37, 39), pm]** 5 times.

> *Use a marker of a different color for beginning-of-round marker.*

Round 1 **[P3, knit to marker]** to end.

Rounds 2 and 4 Knit.

Round 3: Increase round **[P3, slip marker (sm), M1R, knit to marker, M1L, sm]** to end — 2 stitches increased in each section. Work Rounds 1–4 a total of 6 times — **41** (43, **45**, 47, **49**, 51) stitches in each stockinette section.

Section 2 *NEXT 72 ROUNDS*

Rounds 1, 3, and 5 **[P3, knit to marker]** to end.

Rounds 2, 4, 6, and 8 Knit.

Round 7 Work Increase Round. Work Rounds 1–8 a total of 9 times — **59** (61, **63**, 65, **67**, 69) stitches in each stockinette-stitch section.

Section 3 *NEXT 20 ROUNDS*

Rounds 1, 3, 5, and 7 **[P3, knit to marker]** to end.

Rounds 2, 4, 6, 8, and 10 Knit.

Round 9 Work Increase Round. Work Rounds 1–10 twice — **63** (65, **67**, 69, **71**, 73) stitches in each stockinette-stitch section.

Work even until piece measures 23½", or ½" less than desired length.

Rounds 1, 3, and 5 Purl.

Rounds 2 and 4 Knit.

Bind off loosely.

MY LOOK AT IT FROM ALL

angles skirt...

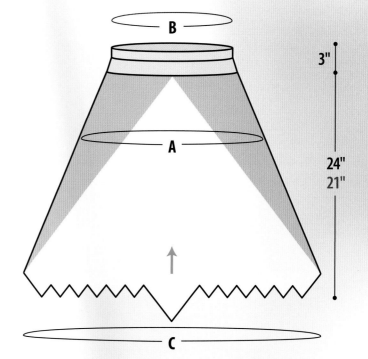

	B	

3"

A

24"
21"

↑

C

shaping

Short-rows panels at sides shape body of skirt.

A 34 (37, 41)"
  36 (**39**, **42**)"

B 28 (31, 34)"
  30 (**33**, **36**)"

C 70"
  70"

finished measurements are for skirt as worn; black numbers show measurements for sock yarn, blue measurements AFTER washing and dying denim yarn

needles

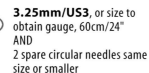

3.25mm/US3, or size to obtain gauge, 60cm/24" AND
2 spare circular needles same size or smaller

3.5mm/E-4

notions

stitch markers

3" repurposed top

gauge

25 stitches

44 rows

in 10cm/4" over garter stitch (after washing and drying denim yarn; see note 2, page 112)

KNIT my SKIRT

Do you want to control your colors, or just go with the flow? With this yarn and these diamonds, you can do either. Work the yarn as it comes, or pull a few yards from the skein until you come to the color you want. Take duo-control!

Miter Gauge

Even with the same stitch/row gauge, yarns will behave differently within miters based on their fiber and drape. Our two 40-stitch miters each measure 4" in width, but the length varies as shown here.

4"

⟨Angles⟩ 5"

4"

⟨Jeans⟩ 4½"

yarn

super fine weight
1525 (1600, **1675**) yds

Shown in Size 34: NORO Taiyo Sock
Yarn in color 17

MITER DIAMOND PANEL

1 Make 7 Basic Miters

Crochet cast on 41 and work Basic Miter (Miter 1). Cut yarn and fasten off. Repeat for Miter 30.

For Miters 2, 4, 7, 17, and 23, do not fasten off; place last stitch on hold.

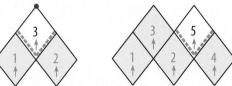

2
Miters 3 and 5 nestle between existing ones; PUK 20 down the left edge of one miter; loop cast on 1; PUK 20 up the right edge of the adjoining miter. After working Miter 5, do not cut yarn; place last stitch on hold and continue with PUK for Miter 6. For Miter 6, PUK 20 down left edge of 5, knit held stitch from 2, then PUK 20 up right edge of 3.

3
Half of the stitches for Miters 8 and 12 are picked up and half are cast on: For Miter 8, PUK 20 down left edge of 7, then cast on 21; for Miter 12, cast on 21, then PUK 20 up right edge of 7.

Work Miters 9, 18, and 24 as for Miter 5 in Step 2; work Miter 13 as for Miter 6 EXCEPT place last stitch on hold; work Miter 31 as for Miter 3.

Following Miter Sequence, continue working miters in order through Miter 37.

4
Turn panel upside down. Skipping first 10 slipped edge stitches, PUK10 along left edge of Miter 1; PUK 1 at join of Miters 1 and 2; PUK10 along right edge of Miter 2. Work Mini Miter (Miter 38). Repeat for Miters 39, 40, 41, 42, and 43.

Repeat Steps 1–4 for second panel.

Continued on page 114

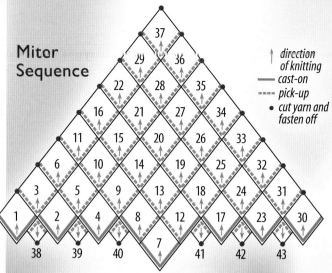

Miter Sequence

↑ *direction of knitting*
— *cast-on*
- - - *pick-up*
● *cut yarn and fasten off*

notes

1 For unfamiliar abbreviations and techniques, see page 116.

2 In the recommended denim yarn, the skirt will shrink about 10% after washing and drying — the pattern takes this shrinkage into account. Be sure to wash and dry your swatch to get an accurate gauge measurement.

3 After weaving in an end of the denim yarn, leave a tail; trim after washing and drying.

Sl 1

Slip stitch purlwise with yarn in front, then move yarn between needle to back of work (do not wrap around side of first stitch).

Center decrease (CD)

On RS Slip 2 together knitwise, k1, p2sso — 2 stitches decreased.
On WS SSPP2 (see page 118) — 2 stitches decreased.

Basic (Mini) miter

Worked over 41 (21) stitches.
Row 1 (WS) Sl 1, k18 (8), SSPP2, k19 (9) — 2 stitches decreased.
Row 2 (RS) Sl 1, k17 (7), Center Decrease (CD), k18 (8) — 2 stitches decreased.
Row 3 Sl 1, k17 (7), p1 (center stitch), k18 (8).
Repeat Rows 2 and 3, working one fewer stitch before and after the CD each RS row.
When 3 stitches remain after a completed RS row, work the last 2 rows as follows:
Last WS row Slip stitch purlwise with yarn in front, p1, k1.
Last RS row CD — 1 stitch remains.
Place last stitch on hold OR cut yarn and fasten off as directed for miter.

...and my Diamonds + Jeans skirt

Color Sequence 1

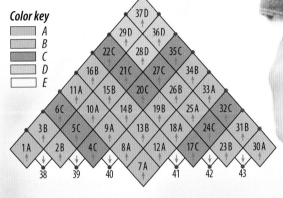

Color key
- A
- B
- C
- D
- E

Work Diamond Miter Panel same as on page 112, EXCEPT follow Color Sequence 1.

yarn

fine weight
2
A 350 (375, **400**) yds
B and C 325 (340, **355**) yds each
D and E 275 (290, **300**) yds each

Shown in Size 36: KOLLAGE YARNS Riveting Sport in colors 7922 Ocean (A), 7904 Charcoal Denim (B), 7913 Raven Denim (C), 7902 Dusk Denim (D), and 7906 Cloud Denim (E)

knit into front & back (kf&b)

1 Knit into front of next stitch on left needle, but do not pull the stitch off the needle.
2 Take right needle to back, then knit through the back of the same stitch.

3 Pull stitch off left needle. Completed increase: 2 stitches from 1 stitch. This increase results in a purl bump after the knit stitch.

SSPP2

A centered double decrease worked on the WS.

1 Slip 2 stitches *separately* to right needle as if to knit.

2 Slip these 2 stitches back onto left needle. Insert right needle through their 'back loops' (into the second stitch and then the first), and slip the 2 stitches to right needle.

3 Purl next stitch.

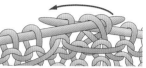

4 Pass 2 slipped stitches over purl stitch and off right needle: 3 stitches become 1; on the right side, the center stitch is on top.

pick up & knit (PUK)

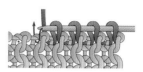

With RS facing and yarn in back, insert needle from front to back in center of edge stitch,

catch yarn, and knit a stitch. (See stockinette left, garter right.)

chain stitch

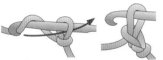

1 Make a slip knot to begin.
2 Catch yarn and draw through loop on hook (left). First chain made (right). Repeat Step 2.

SSK

A left-slanting single decrease

1 Slip 2 stitches separately to right needle as if to knit.

2 Slip left needle into these 2 stitches from left to right and knit them together:

2 stitches become 1.

short rows (W&T)

Each short row adds two rows of knitting across a section of the work. Since the work is turned before completing a row, stitches must be wrapped at the turn to prevent holes. On stockinette stitch, work a wrap as follows:

Knit side

1 With yarn in back, slip next stitch as if to purl. Bring yarn to front of work and slip stitch back to left needle (as shown). Turn work.
2 With yarn in front, slip next stitch as if to purl. Work to end.

3 When you come to the wrap on a following knit row, hide the wrap by knitting it together with the stitch it wraps.

Purl side

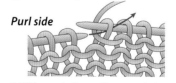

1 With yarn in front, slip next stitch as if to purl. Bring yarn to back of work and slip stitch back to left needle (as shown). Turn work.
2 With yarn in back, slip next stitch as if to purl. Work to end.

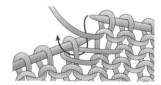

3 When you come to the wrap on a following purl row, hide the wrap by purling it together with the stitch it wraps.

k2tog (k3tog)

A right-slanting single (double) decrease

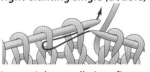

1 Insert right needle into first 2 (3) stitches on left needle, beginning with second (third) stitch from end of left needle.

2 Knit these 2 (3) stitches together as if they were 1.

p2tog (p3tog)

A right-slanting single (double) decrease

1 Insert right needle into first 2 (3) stitches on left needle.

2 Purl these 2 (3) stitches together as if they were 1.

make 1 (M1)

M1L

For a *left-slanting* increase, insert left needle from front to back under strand between last stitch knitted and first stitch on left needle. Knit, twisting strand by working into loop at back of needle.

The result is a left-slanting increase.

M1R

Or, for a *right-slanting* increase, insert left needle from back to front under strand between last stitch knitted and first stitch on left needle. Knit, twisting strand by working into loop at front of needle.

The result is a right-slanting increase.

M1P

For a *purl* increase, insert left needle from front to back under strand between last stitch worked and first stitch on left needle. Purl, twisting strand by working into loop at back of needle from left to right.

grafting

Stockinette-stitch graft:

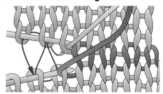

An invisible method of joining knitting horizontally, row to row. Also called Kitchener stitch.

CONVERSION CHART

centimeters	0.394	inches
grams	0.035	ounces
inches	2.54	centimeters
ounces	28.6	grams
meters	1.1	yards
yards	.91	meters

EQUIVALENT WEIGHTS

¾	oz	20 g
1	oz	28 g
1½	oz	40 g
1¾	oz	50 g
2	oz	57 g
3½	oz	100 g

abbreviations

CC contrasting color
cm centimeter(s)
dec decrease
g gram(s)
" inch(es)
inc increase
k knit
LH left-hand
M1 make one stitch (increase)
m meter(s)
mm millimeter(s)
MC main color
oz ounce(s)
p purl
pm place marker
psso pass slipped stitch(es) over
RH right-hand
RS right side(s)
sl slip
SKP slip, knit, psso
SK2P slip, k2tog, psso
ssk slip, slip, knit these 2 sts tog
ssp slip, slip, purl these 2 sts tog
st(s) stitch(es)
tbl through back of loop(s)
tog together
WS wrong side(s)
x times
yd(s) yard(s)
yo yarn over

Project yarns

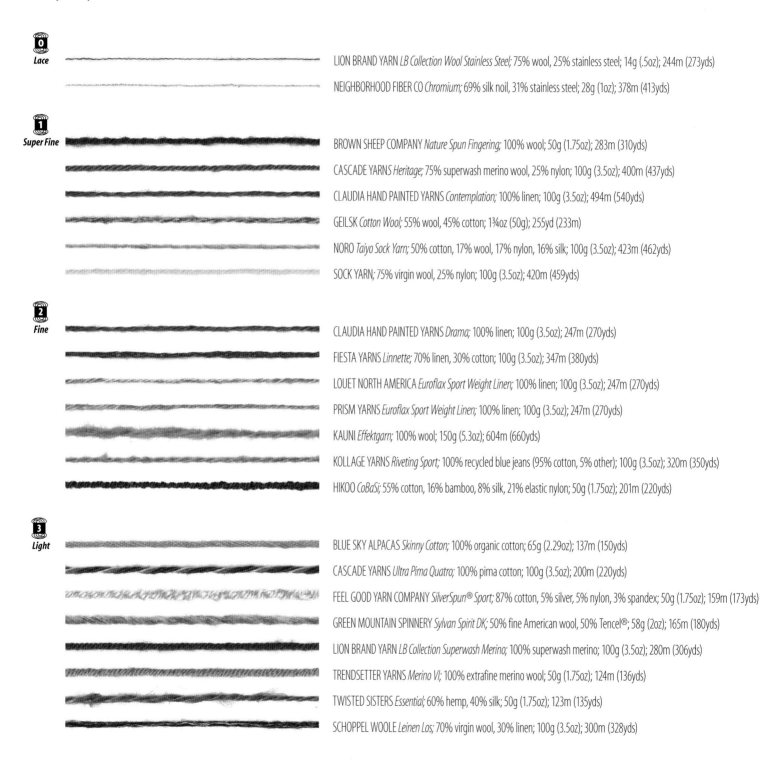

0 Lace

LION BRAND YARN *LB Collection Wool Stainless Steel*; 75% wool, 25% stainless steel; 14g (.5oz); 244m (273yds)

NEIGHBORHOOD FIBER CO *Chromium*; 69% silk noil, 31% stainless steel; 28g (1oz); 378m (413yds)

1 Super Fine

BROWN SHEEP COMPANY *Nature Spun Fingering*; 100% wool; 50g (1.75oz); 283m (310yds)

CASCADE YARNS *Heritage*; 75% superwash merino wool, 25% nylon; 100g (3.5oz); 400m (437yds)

CLAUDIA HAND PAINTED YARNS *Contemplation*; 100% linen; 100g (3.5oz); 494m (540yds)

GEILSK *Cotton Wool*; 55% wool, 45% cotton; 1¾oz (50g); 255yd (233m)

NORO *Taiyo Sock Yarn*; 50% cotton, 17% wool, 17% nylon, 16% silk; 100g (3.5oz); 423m (462yds)

SOCK YARN; 75% virgin wool, 25% nylon; 100g (3.5oz); 420m (459yds)

2 Fine

CLAUDIA HAND PAINTED YARNS *Drama*; 100% linen; 100g (3.5oz); 247m (270yds)

FIESTA YARNS *Linnette*; 70% linen, 30% cotton; 100g (3.5oz); 347m (380yds)

LOUET NORTH AMERICA *Euroflax Sport Weight Linen*; 100% linen; 100g (3.5oz); 247m (270yds)

PRISM YARNS *Euroflax Sport Weight Linen*; 100% linen; 100g (3.5oz); 247m (270yds)

KAUNI *Effektgarn*; 100% wool; 150g (5.3oz); 604m (660yds)

KOLLAGE YARNS *Riveting Sport*; 100% recycled blue jeans (95% cotton, 5% other); 100g (3.5oz); 320m (350yds)

HIKOO *CoBaSi*; 55% cotton, 16% bamboo, 8% silk, 21% elastic nylon; 50g (1.75oz); 201m (220yds)

3 Light

BLUE SKY ALPACAS *Skinny Cotton*; 100% organic cotton; 65g (2.29oz); 137m (150yds)

CASCADE YARNS *Ultra Pima Quatro*; 100% pima cotton; 100g (3.5oz); 200m (220yds)

FEEL GOOD YARN COMPANY *SilverSpun® Sport*; 87% cotton, 5% silver, 5% nylon, 3% spandex; 50g (1.75oz); 159m (173yds)

GREEN MOUNTAIN SPINNERY *Sylvan Spirit DK*; 50% fine American wool, 50% Tencel®; 58g (2oz); 165m (180yds)

LION BRAND YARN *LB Collection Superwash Merino*; 100% superwash merino; 100g (3.5oz); 280m (306yds)

TRENDSETTER YARNS *Merino VI*; 100% extrafine merino wool; 50g (1.75oz); 124m (136yds)

TWISTED SISTERS *Essential*; 60% hemp, 40% silk; 50g (1.75oz); 123m (135yds)

SCHOPPEL WOOLE *Leinen Los*; 70% virgin wool, 30% linen; 100g (3.5oz); 300m (328yds)

CANDACE skirts

Yarn weight categories

0	**1**	**2**	**3**	**4**
lace	*super fine*	*fine*	*light*	*medium*

Also called

Fingering	Sock	Sport	DK	Worsted
10-count	Fingering	Baby	Light-	Afghan
Crochet Thread	Baby		Worsted	Aran

Stockinette Stitch Gauge Range 10cm/4 inches

33 sts	27 sts	23 sts	21 sts	16 sts
to	to	to	to	to
40 sts	32 sts	26 sts	24 sts	20 sts

Recommended needle (metric)

1.5 mm	2.25 mm	3.25 mm	3.75 mm	4.5 mm
to	to	to	to	to
2.25mm	3.25 mm	3.75 mm	4.5 mm	5.5 mm

Recommended needle (US)

000 to 1	1 to 3	3 to 5	5 to 7	7 to 9r

Locate the Yarn Weight and Stockinette Stitch Gauge Range over 10cm to 4" on the chart. Compare that range with the information on the yarn label to find an appropriate yarn.

These are guidelines only for commonly used gauges and needle sizes in specific yarn categories.

Supplier list

BLUE SKY ALPACAS, INC.
PO Box 88
Cedar, MN 55011
(888) 460-8862
www.blueskyalpacas.com

BROWN SHEEP COMPANY
100662 County Road 16
Mitchell, NE 69357
(800) 826-9136
www.brownsheep.com

CASCADE YARNS®
www.cascadeyarns.com

CLAUDIA HAND PAINTED YARNS
40 West Washington St
Harrisonburg, VA 22802
(540) 433-1140
www.claudiaco.com

FEEL GOOD YARN COMPANY®
3419 Morrison St. NW
Washington DC 20015
(202) 309-2546
www.feelgoodyarnco.com

FIESTA YARNS
5620 Venice Ave NE, Suite J
Albuquerque, NM 87113
(505) 892-5008
www.fiestayarns.com

GEILSK YARNS
distributed by Tutto Santa Fe
10 Domingo Road
Santa Fe, NM 87508
(505) 466-4326
www.knit-geilsk.com

GREEN MOUNTAIN SPINNERY
PO Box 568
Putney, VT 05346-0568
(800) 321-9665
www.spinnery.com

HIKOO
distributed by Skacel Collection, Inc
PO Box 88110
Seattle, WA 98138-2110
(800) 255-1278
www.skacelknitting.com

KAUNI
distributed by RYN Yarn
308 Pine Street
Sheboygan Falls, WI 53085
(920) 467-9948

KOLLAGE YARNS
3591 Cahaba Beach Road
Birmingham, AL 35242
(888) 829-7758
www.kollageyarns.com

LION BRAND YARNS
135 Kero Road
Carlstadt, NJ 07072
(201) 804-3999
www.lionbrand.com

LOUET NORTH AMERICA
3425 Hands Road
Prescott, ON, Canada K0E 1T0
(800) 897-6444
www.louet.com

NEIGHBORHOOD FIBER CO
700 N Eutaw St
Baltimore, MD 21201
(401) 989-3770
www.neighborhoodfiberco.com

NORO
distributed by Knitting Fever, Inc
315 Bayview Avenue
Amityville, NY 11701
(800) 645-3457
www.knittingfever.com

PRISM ARTS
3140 39th Ave N
St Petersburg, FL 33714
(727) 528-3800
www.prismyarn.com

SCHOPPEL WOLLE
distributed by Skacel Collection, Inc
PO Box 88110
Seattle, WA 98138-2110
(800) 255-1278
www.skacelknitting.com

TRENDSETTER YARNS
16745 Saticoy St, Suite 101
Van Nuys, CA 91406
(818) 780-5497
www.trendsetteryarns.com

TWISTED SISTERS
available at Great Yarns
4023 Rucker Ave
Everett, WA 98201
(425) 252-8155
www.greatyarns.com

acknowledgements

A bravo to my dear friends ○ who helped me with the knitting:
Lois Mitchell and Connie Burmeister.

About twenty years ago someone gave me a small green pamphlet about a knitting event that was called Stitches. Little did I know that this booklet would be the catalyst to shaping my future career in knitting. As I browsed through the pages I noticed many names that I recognized from knitting books and published patterns. I loved knitting and designing, and I decided that I wanted to be one of those people. With my cello in one hand and my knitting in the other, I embarked upon a double-career tug of war. Eventually my knitting hand won.

This book is the highlight of my knitting career. For a writer, words are tools. One would think it would be easy to express sincere thanks to all the people who worked so hard to make this dream a reality, but it is difficult. I will try.

Karen — You are the most organized person I know, and you kept things moving at a smooth pace, always with good humor and patience. You solved problems before I could voice them.

Carol — Your technical drawings are things of beauty and usefulness, translating my sometimes unorthodox techniques into step-by-step directions that knitters all over will appreciate, as I do.

Sarah — You quietly crunched millions of numbers that would make an ordinary person (like me) scream with frustration, without a single e-mail peep or squawk.

Natalie — You have the artistic ability of a Dutch master, a talent for choosing colors that would make Van Gogh envious, and the knack of mixing it all with enchanting whimsy. *Knit My Skirt* was a title of brilliance.

Denny — You are a computer mastermind who sees color and makes it true and rich.

Rick — You are an astonishing knitter-and-a-half…half physicist, half artist, half extraordinary knitting-solutions technician. Your sketches and insight continually taught me new things, and your styling made my skirts look gorgeous. And I thought *my* mind worked in weird ways!

Benjamin — You gave me opportunities and support throughout it all. CEO can also stand for Candace Experiences Opportunity, thanks to you.

Ken — You are my husband of infinite patience. You are my life's accompanist.

My three sons: Nathaniel, Liam, and Noah — They finally think I'm cool.

My knitting colleagues — You lift me up every time I see you, laughing about lost luggage or airport sleep-ins, and justifying that our work is important to knitters everywhere.

And the two people who are 2/3 of the XRX logo:

Elaine — Thoughtful, thorough, and persuasive, you led the team that edited my wayward words into clear and cohesive thoughts, and turned my skirt patterns into concise blueprints. Thank you for lighting and carrying the torch that will make people believe that knitting skirts is fun and easy, and that everyone can wear and look great in one.

Alexis — It is here that words fail me, but pictures speak volumes. Thank you for your photographs — they turned my humble work into works of art.

PHOTO BY LISA MANNES

A standing ovation to all the wonderfully generous yarn companies
and the people there who were all so friendly and gracious.

31901063937751

LENNY THE LIGHTHOUSE FINDS A DOLLAR
Book II

LENNY DECIDES WHAT TO DO

Written by Dana Fennie

Illustrated by Bella Maher

For his unwavering support, and encouragement,
I dedicate this series of books to
Walter Blackmon.

Special thanks to Kenli, Amelia and Georgia,
for my constant and ongoing motivation.

Copyright TXu 2-252-327 2005 All rights reserved. Conceived, written, edited,
financed, assembled, digitized, formatted and printed in the United States of
America. No part of this book may be reproduced, copied, transmitted, or stored
in any form or by any means, graphic, electronic, or mechanical, including
photocopying, taping, and recording without prior written permission from the
copyright owner. ISBN #978-1-7370246-4-4

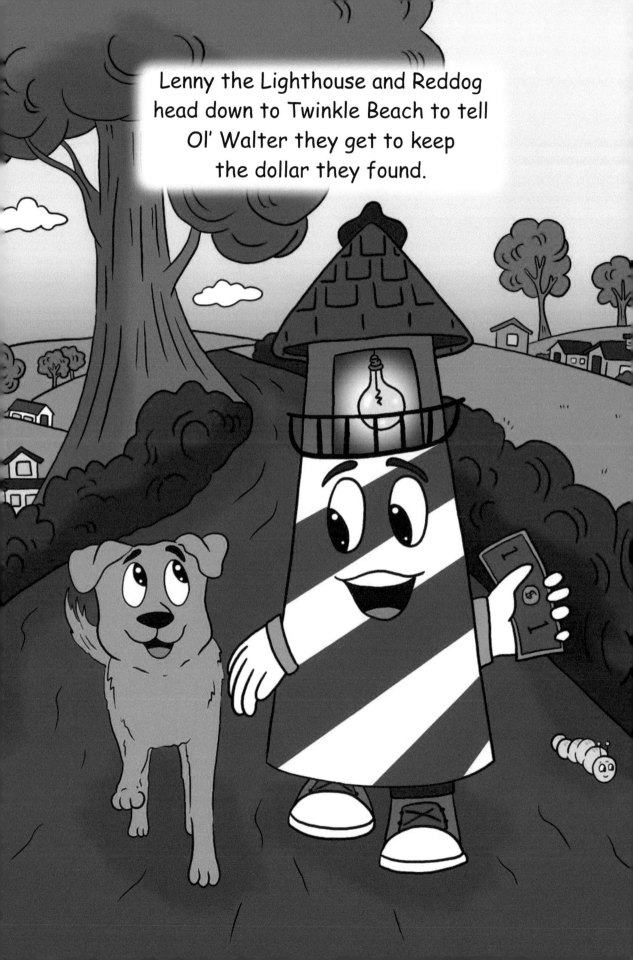

On their way to the beach
they passed by Mr. Ryan
working behind his store.

"Why are you throwing these
things away?" asked Lenny.

"These are old damaged
things I can't sell anymore,"
said Mr. Ryan.

"These are pretty neat!" exclaimed Lenny,
as he held up a small green jar to look
through. "It makes the whole world look
green!" Reddog liked it too.

Lenny asked Mr. Ryan
if he could have a couple of the jars
that he was throwing away.

"Sure, but you have to take them all,"
said Mr. Ryan.

"Wow! That's great Mr. Ryan!
Thank you!" said Lenny.

"Oh boy, come on Reddog! Let's go ask my mom if we can keep the jars," said Lenny.

"Ok," sighed Lenny's mom. "But if they get in my way I'm going to throw them out!"
"Oh Mom!" said Lenny. "I'll keep them in the shed and out of your way."
"Ok, that will work," agreed Lenny's mom.
Thanks Mom!" said Lenny.

Lenny and Reddog dropped off the wagon
full of jars in the shed,
then they went out to Twinkle Beach
to tell Ol' Walter all their exciting news.

Lenny and Reddog decided to play on the beach until Ol' Walter woke up.

They looked at the world through their colored jars.

Just then, Ol' Walter woke up.
"Well well, it's my good friends
Lenny the Lighthouse and Reddog."

"Hi Walter!" said Lenny. We just came
from Officer Ronnie and guess what?"
"Well I don't know, what?"
said Walter.

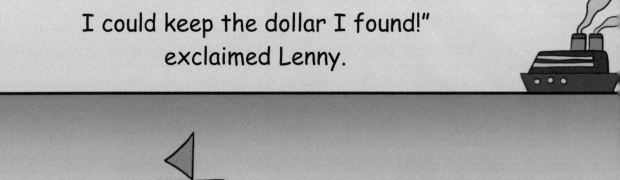

"Officer Ronnie said
I could keep the dollar I found!"
exclaimed Lenny.

"That is great news!" agreed Walter. "What are you going to do with all that money?"

"I don't know," said Lenny.

"What should I do with my money?"

"Well," said Walter. "Having money is a great responsibility, no matter how much you have.

When it comes to money you should always,

save a little, give a little, spend a little."

"Get in the habit of saving money now,
while you are young,
then you will always have money when
you need it!"

"Save a little, give a little, spend a little. That's great!" said Lenny. "Thanks Walter!

But right now I have to get home to do my homework. I'll see you later."

After dinner Lenny put his dollar in his piggy bank.
Lenny laid in bed thinking about his money,
and what he could do with it.
He would save half, like Ol' Walter said,
but Lenny felt he should also do
something good with his dollar.

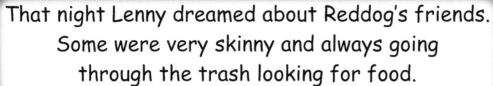

That night Lenny dreamed about Reddog's friends.
Some were very skinny and always going
through the trash looking for food.

They're hungry,
I can help them!
That's what I'll do,
thought Lenny.

In the morning, Lenny counted all the coins in his piggy bank. It added up to two dollars and seven cents. "I'm going to do just like Ol' Walter said. I'll save one dollar and seven cents, and help Reddog's friends with the rest of the money."

After breakfast, Lenny stopped by
Mr. Ryan's store to buy some food.

Lenny told Mr. Ryan what he wanted to do.
Mr. Ryan sold Lenny all the food
he could for one dollar.

"I'm afraid that won't feed very many friends,"
said Mr. Ryan.

"You're right" said Lenny.
"But if I can help just one friend,
that will be better than doing nothing!"

"Right you are," agreed Mr. Ryan.

Lenny asked Reddog which of his friends was the hungriest?

"I have a lot of hungry friends," said Reddog,
"but Izzy probably needs it the most."
He is small, and getting older.

"OK," said Lenny, "Izzy is the one I want to help!"

"Hi Izzy," said Reddog.
"This is my friend Lenny, and he has a gift for you!"
"Great," said Izzy sleepily.
"But I'm so tired and hungry I can hardly move."

"That's just it!" said Lenny.
"I brought you some food!"
"For me?" asked Izzy.
"Wow, thank you Lenny!
I'm going to share this with my
friend Daisy, she is hungry too."

"Hi Daisy! This is my friend Lenny the Lighthouse.
He has brought us some food!" said Izzy.

Lenny, Reddog, Izzy, and Daisy
were so happy! They all hugged, and jumped,
and danced around together.
And they sang, "Thank you Lenny the Lighthouse!"

On their way home, Lenny told Reddog that helping his friends made him feel really good inside.

Lenny decided he wanted to feed more hungry dogs, cats, and friends.

"Let's go ask Ol' Walter how we can make some more money," said Lenny.

"I'm not even sure where money really comes from."

THE END

What would you do to make some money to help Reddogs's friends?

Lessons Learned:

Always get permission first: Lenny asked Mr. Ryan for the jars. Lenny asked his mom if he can keep the jars in the shed.

Save a little, give a little, spend a little: Lenny saved $1.07 in his piggy bank. He bought some food, then gave the food to Izzy and Daisy.

Think before you do something: Lenny thought about what he wanted to do with the money.

Friendships are special: Lenny and Reddog are special friends.

Always do your homework or chores first: Homework and chores are your responsibilities. Responsibilities always come first, before anything else. Lenny had to get home to do his homework.

Giving: Even if it's just a little bit, it's better to give than to receive. Lenny only had two cans of food, but it still felt good to see Izzy and Daisy so happy.

Sharing: Even though he only had a little bit, Izzy immediately shared his food with his friend Daisy.

Don't be afraid to ask someone you know for help or advice: Most people are happy to help. Lenny looks to Ol' Walter for advice.

This is Millimeter the inchworm. I call him Meter.

How many Meters can you find… I found 10

Be sure to visit www.lennythelighthouse.com for news and updates.